SARAH WAGNER

Destiny Awaits Devo

A Companion Guide to Awakening of the Giants

First edition

This book was professionally typeset on Reedsy.
Find out more at reedsy.com

Can you not discern this new day of destiny breaking forth around you? The early signs of my purposes and plans are bursting forth. The budding vines of new life are now blooming everywhere. The fragrance of their flowers whispers, "There is change in the air." Arise, my love, my beautiful companion, and run with me to the higher place. For now is the time to arise and come away with me.

Song of Songs 2:13 (TPT)

Contents

Foreword

When I set out to write *Awakening of the Giants*, I had no idea where it would take me. The whole idea started as the brainchild of my youngest son, Samuel, who gave me the inspiration. I thought, "How fun to write a book with my son?" What he didn't tell me was that I would be solely writing the book, and he would be happy to inspire me.

"See, God knew what it would take my son to get my fingers moving." God had destined that I would eventually write. I've always loved writing. I've actually been hired to ghostwrite and edit. Yet, I never thought of it as my passion nor my destiny. God knew that I wouldn't be able to pass up the opportunity to connect with my son on a fun adventure. What mother wouldn't want to do anything within their power for their child?

As I sat at my computer, the ideas just began to flow. I knew very little about giants and dragons. I don't think I've ever even read a fantasy fiction book, other than one of the Narnia books to my children. I barely knew what fantasy fiction was.

Yet, God knew. He had already prepared me for this venture in my past experiences and interests. God doesn't want any of our talents or experiences to go to waste. So, as I pressed into Him for wisdom and insight, the plot and story began to unfold. Often times as I prayed, He would reveal images that would direct me to my next chapter. He is the best antidote for writer's block and, in fact, the whole purpose for writing.

My life verse is Jeremiah 29:11 (NLT)...

"For I know the plans I have for you," says the Lord. "They are plans for good and not for disaster, to give you a future and a hope.

Since I was a small child, I have known the Lord and have never doubted that

Jesus is my very reason for being. Whatever hardships I have gone through, Jesus has been there. My biggest decisions in life came through his guidance. My biggest victories came because of him. Amid my hardships, he was there and still is, leading and steering my life.

I pray that you will utilize this devotional to press into all that the Lord has for you. I encourage you to find your "Band of Brothers" or "Band of Sisters" to lean and grow with as you read *Awakening of the Giants* and follow along with the *Destiny Awaits Devo.*

As you discover all that God has for you, I pray that you will not be afraid of whatever challenge comes your way. May your imagination soar and your heart dance as you press into God's big plan for you. I can promise you, it is so much bigger than what you could ever hope or imagine.

That doesn't mean that pursuing your destiny will be easy or trouble-free. It just means that God is with you, and He will provide you with all that you need to take you on His big adventure specially designed for you.

As you read through the *Awakening of the Giants,* you will see the alternative to the Prophecy, otherwise known as the Curse. You see, Satan has a plan for your life as well. Let's be real, the Devil wants to destroy us. His plans for us are to not only settle for what the world has given us and accept our lot in life—but to utterly decimate us. We must be ready for both. And be prepared to fight as your destiny awaits.

A thief has only one thing in mind—he wants to steal, slaughter, and destroy. But I have come to give you everything in abundance, more than you expect—life in its fullness until you overflow!

John 10:10 (TPT)

Preface

SPOILER ALERT!
This devotional includes excerpts from
Awakening of the Giants!

```
Please read the corresponding chapter FIRST to not spoil the
details.
```

Awakening of the Giants is an allegory that draws a beautiful illustration of life and the cataclysmic fight between good and evil that we face every day. This guide is designed to accompany you as you battle the war of the worlds. Socrates said, "An unexamined life is not worth living." This is a quote that I try to live by, and you will come to understand all too well by the time you are done.

You will be challenged to deeply search your heart and take a journey into your life from childhood until now, and then moving forward. This is your story! You are the main character, and it's all about YOU! You can fly solo or invite your small group, friends, or family to join you. Whomever you decide to voyage with, whatever age or group, be sure that you can be real and transparent in a safe environment as you dig deep into the recesses of your heart and soul, and they dive into theirs.

Feel free to fill in the blanks and share them with your group as you grow together in pursuing your destiny. However, if you decide not to fill in the answers, I strongly encourage you to at least write out your answers in the

"Destiny Question" section. When completed, you will have a record of the Prophecy written in your heart.

How much do we grow in our walk as we share our hearts?

Love empowers us to fulfill the law of the Anointed One as we carry each other's troubles. Gal. 6:2 (TPT)

As we meet together with united hearts and souls, caring for one another's burdens, we are walking out our faith. Jesus already knows our troubles, but he has given us each other as well to help in our triumphs and trials. I encourage you to build your "Band", those that help you reach your destiny in Christ. As you ask the Lord to reveal whom they may be, He will show you. My "Band" in this venture is my family. My husband and my four sons enjoy our weekly *Destiny Awaits Devo* as we open our hearts and souls in meaningful time jointly. Even though my boys are grown, they are eager to band together, and a scrumptious meal to follow only sweetens the experience.

Whomever your Band, you will find the reading of *Awakening of the Giants*, combined with the *Destiny Awaits Devos*, will knit your hearts and souls together as you pursue your destiny together as a Band.

Whether you know Jesus or not, He knows you and longs to help you fulfill your destiny, passionately pleading before God for us. How amazing is that? If you want to be sure that you have invited Jesus into your Awakening, just head to the "Destiny Awaits Prayer" section in the back of this book where you can invite Jesus to join you on your life adventure. See God, the creator of the universe, has already searched your heart, and He knows you fully. He understands the deepest desires of your heart.

"Yet he also understands the desires of the Spirit, because the Holy Spirit passionately pleads before God for us, his holy ones, in perfect harmony with God's plan and our destiny." Rom. 8:27 (TPT)

How can it get any better than that? "El Roi," the God who sees me, has a perfect plan for your life and destiny. The sooner you pursue that plan—the better. Once we know Christ, we receive this inheritance that was plotted out before we were even born.

Before we were even born, he gave us our destiny; that we would fulfill the plan of God who always accomplishes every purpose and plan in his heart. Ephesians

1:11 (TPT)

God's plan for you is just waiting. What's so amazing is that God's plan is even bigger than our plans. It's so much greater than we can imagine. He actually commissions us as his assistants!

Get up and stand to your feet, for I have appeared to you to reveal your destiny and to commission you as my assistant. You will be a witness to what you have seen and to the things I will reveal whenever I appear to you. Acts 26:16 (TPT)

There is much work to be done, and the Devil rages, as he knows his days are short. It's time to heed our calling and follow in His plan for our lives. Our days are but a mist, and there is no time to waste. As Exijah says, "Time is of the essence, but indeed, you need to think this through and unite in your decision.... The days are becoming dark, and we do not know what the future holds."

```
What is your destiny?
What is your calling?
```

Then you will discover all that is just, proper, and fair and be empowered to make the right decisions as you walk into your destiny. Proverbs 2:9 (TPT)

Things never discovered or heard of before,
*   things beyond our ability to imagine—*
these are the many things God has in store
*   for all his lovers. I Cor. 2:9 (TPT)*

"'The Great Awakening' will bring about the rising of the giants in our land.
This day will be either a day of doom or celebration,
depending on if you can break the Curse and fulfill the Prophecy or not.
Destiny is in your hands."

Acknowledgement

Dedicated to all the spiritual leaders in my life.

My big brother, who took me to church on the bus when I was just four. This is where I met the Lord.

My mother, who taught me about Jesus.

My Sunday school teachers, who made sure I knew the Word of God.

My dear, lifelong friend and youth group leader, who went way beyond her calling, still walking with me—in faith and life.

My band of sisters in so many spaces and places, who I can call and pray and connect with at any time, even if we haven't talked in months.

My Band of Boys, including my husband and four sons, who bring such incredible encouragement to my heart and soul.

To all those who have helped me reach my destiny. God's not finished with me yet, but I am on my way.

Thank you to all for being a light that shined into my life!

The Journey

It is the Lord who directs your life,
for each step you take is ordained by God
to bring you closer to your destiny.
So much of your life, then, remains a mystery!
Proverbs 20:24 (TPT)

A rchin traveled home on his daily route when he heard a scream. Having no idea what he would encounter, he pulled over and found a beautiful baby boy. What a surprise for someone who thought he would be childless.

* * *

The Band of Brothers headed to the slope to play their favorite game, "King of the Mountain." No doubt they had played this game a thousand times in their growing-up years, but suddenly they lost sight of several of their friends. Not knowing if they were in harm's way or perhaps even plunged to their death, they were startled.

Indeed, the journey of life can take us on some perilous trails. Some we choose not to remember but, sadly can never forget. Others we forget, but ironically, wish we could remember. Whatever the case, you must know that

Jesus has always been there for you. In this guide, we will often go back to our childhood because it has led us to where we are. No matter how old we get, it all started somewhere on that mountain slope playing "King of the Mountain."

Whether you knew Jesus as a child, or still feel like you do not know him, Jesus was there and still is there. He is longing to be a part of your journey. It's never too early or too late to invite the "Light of the World" into your story and change the ending. For all the moments you did not know Him, you can still invite Him to put those painful memories to rest.

Destiny Chats:

What was your favorite childhood game/activity, and what did you love about it?

What do you do for leisure now, and what do you love about it?

Share one of the biggest surprises in your life.
How did it make you feel?

We've all had times in our life that have led us to the unexpected, perhaps daily.
Can you share about an unexpected occurrence in your life?

Can you share a time when a certain out-of-the-ordinary event changed your life forever?

Sometimes, it's hard to see God's hand in the midst of an unexpected event, especially when it's difficult, but as we look back, we can see God's hand at work.

How can you see God's hand in this extraordinary event?

Destiny Question:

This is your time to roar! What are some of your dreams, whether fulfilled or unfulfilled?

Destiny Prayer:

Lord, I invite you into my journey today. Would you please direct my life and guide each step, that I may draw closer to my destiny? Thank you that I'm not alone.
    In Jesus' name, amen.

Destiny Notes:

The Curse

Nevertheless, the Curse lived on—directing their very way of life. The townsfolk failed to realize that the destruction wreaked by the giants had not only devastated their land but also decimated their hearts.

Nonetheless, Goggen was their home, and none could convince them otherwise. Moreover, since they dared not venture beyond their borders, they could not even begin to comprehend that there was any other way of living ... It was truly the tale of two lands.

Goggen had four villages—all bearing the bastion of consequences left by the wretched Curse. Krindel, Winchin, Mushkin, and Zolar were connected by the mountains but disconnected by their brokenness. Their mere existence was enough to keep them plodding along ... yet purpose was not an object to be pondered.

* * *

Have you ever wondered why so many people settle into their misery? Do they not realize that they live on the edge of despair, or is it that they have grown complacent in their sorrow? "Misery loves company" isn't too far from the truth when you realize how many of us just grow comfortable doing the same insane tactics that only lead to greater suffering.

"People of the Lie" could be the title of their book, perhaps? These are those who continue to make the same bad choices and somehow imagine that life will eventually get better. It is believed that Einstein once said, "the definition of insanity is doing the same thing repeatedly and expecting a different result."

Yet in Romans 7, we find that even the Apostle Paul fell prey to this insidious behavior.

I want to do what is good, but I don't. I don't want to do what is wrong, but I do it anyway. Romans 7:19 (NLT)

So we ask ourselves, why do I continue to do the things I don't want to do that lead to more devastating consequences?

The Goggenites wallowed in their sorrow and misery yet never dared to venture out to see if there was a better way of life. It seems odd, yet this is how many choose to live whether intentionally or unintentionally. The fear of the unknown can truly be crippling. How easy it is to settle into complacency with the familiar, not realizing that we have lost vision and hope ....

Destiny Chats:

Can you think of a movie or book that you have read where one of the characters settles for less? What do you want to tell that character?

Do you know someone from your past that had such great potential yet didn't live up to it?
   What was the scenario? Without naming this person, what would you say to them if you could?

How about someone who you who did not see great potential in yet achieved great success?

Why do you think this person succeeded?

What do you think made the difference between those who didn't realize their potential and those who fulfilled their potential?

What are some positive behaviors/habits that you have incorporated into your life that have made a positive difference?

Destiny Question:

Jesus came to reverse the curse of sin and death. What are you settling for that is keeping you from all that God has for you?

Destiny Prayer:

Lord, would you catch me when I'm falling? Thank you for your grace.

You hear me when I'm calling. Don't let me fall back in those chains.

You're my saving grace. You're my secret place. When I was lost in space, you made a way.

Don't let me go. Don't let me go.

I love you.

In Jesus' name, amen.[1]

Destiny Notes:

Destiny

Today I have given you the choice between life and death,
between blessings and curses.
Now I call on heaven and earth to witness the choice you make.
Oh, that you would choose life, so that you and your descendants might live!
Deuteronomy 30:19 (NLT)

"'The Great Awakening' will bring about the rising of the giants. This day will be either a day of doom or celebration—depending on if you can break the Curse and fulfill the Prophecy or not. Destiny is in your hands."

* * *

The Prophecy or the Curse, as destiny awaits? The Band of Brothers stumbled across the hidden Prophecy that would break the Curse, and they had to make a choice. Would they fulfill the Prophecy and break the Curse or wait for someone else to rise up? It seemed so blatant ... They were the Chosen.

Have you ever come across a major crossroads in your life where you had to make a choice that would affect not just your future but others? Unfortunately, these tend to be the most difficult decisions.

I have had my fair share of opportunities where the sensitive information I was given had to be conveyed to the proper authorities. In doing so, the outcome was destined to affect many, and not necessarily in a positive manner.

The stress can be unbearable, and giving it to God was the only method that worked for me. I knew that if I stood on truth, I had nothing to fear as I walked in faith. Did that mean that I did not waver as Satan attacked me with lies? Absolutely not. It meant that I had to stand ready for battle, clothing myself with the armor of God, no matter how difficult the circumstances.

As I move forward in life, I realize that every day allows choices that shape our destiny as we choose the Prophecy or the Curse, thus, affecting not just ourselves, but others.

Some may seem innocent at the time but later yield a detrimental outcome that devastates hearts and souls—The information we share with others that may or may not be gossip? How about the tone we use with our loved ones that has the power to bring life or bring death? The use of our time or talents can be our downfall … Are we squandering the gifts given by God through idleness? Do we love well? Are we neglecting the least of these?

So, whether you eat or drink, or whatever you do, do it all for the glory of God. I Corinthians 10:31 (NIV)

This sure seems like a tough standard when we analyze our daily choices, but if we are called to live out our destiny in all that God has for us, this is where it begins.

The reality is that, in many ways, we write our own stories. God is the author, but we are the editors. Our daily decisions map out our lives. It's easy to blame God or others when our choices lead to unintended consequences, but do we ever consider the part we play?

Here's the first bad decision made in our world today. Adam and Even had two choices, eat from the trees of the garden, or the tree of the knowledge of good and evil. It seemed like it was so easy for them to avoid that one tree. There were so many other trees, beautiful trees—overflowing with succulent fruit. How is it they were taken in by that one tree? The tree of knowledge of good and evil that was right there in the middle of the garden. Since that time, we have all suffered because of their bad decision.

The Lord God took the man and put him in the garden of Eden to work it and keep it. And the Lord God commanded the man, saying, "You may surely eat of every tree of the garden, but of the tree of the knowledge of good and evil you shall not eat, for in the day that you eat of it you shall surely die." Gen 2: 15 (NLT)

And everything I've taught you is so that the peace which is in me will be in you and will give you great confidence as you rest in me. For in this unbelieving world you will experience trouble and sorrows, but you must be courageous, for I have conquered the world! John 16:33 (TPT)

As we go through life, we have many choices. Just like Adam and Eve, we can choose the trees of the garden or the tree of knowledge of good and evil. The trees in the garden lead to life. The tree of the knowledge of good and evil leads to death. Which tree are you eating from?

Destiny Chats:

What are a few of the best decisions you have made?

How did you arrive at your decision/decisions?

What was the consequence?

Can you share about the most overwhelming task that you have taken on in your life?
What was the outcome?

What about a not-so-good decision? What was the consequence?

What do you want the next chapter of your life to look like?

Destiny Questions:

What is your 'Tree of Life'—meaning where do you turn for life and vitality?

What is your 'Tree of Death'—meaning what temptation is lurking in your garden that you know will crush your heart and soul?

Destiny Prayer:

Dear Lord, today, I choose life over death. I choose the Prophecy over the Curse. I choose to celebrate the victory you have had in my life, and I await the writing of the next chapter with you as the Author and Editor of my story.

In Jesus' name, amen.

Destiny Notes:

The Chosen

A person may have many ideas concerning God's plan for his life,
but only the designs of God's purpose will succeed in the end.
Proverbs 19:21 (TPT)

"**A**s I told your dear precious sons in the heart of the mine, the Prophecy awaits to be fulfilled. Your boys have been chosen from almost one thousand years ago to—not only set the Land of Goggen free—but save the Land of Olaquin."

* * *

The Band of Brothers had each been chosen to break the Curse even before they were born. They were the ones to crush the darkness and shine the light. In much the same way, when you come to Christ, you enter into his family as a chosen people. You are called out of darkness and into his marvelous light long before you are born.

Imagine picking up a book called "The Chosen," and it's all about your life as you walk into the plan that God laid out just for you? That's the story that God is calling you to. He has intricately planned a future for you that only you can fulfill as you pursue your destiny in Him. Doesn't this sound like the most amazing novel ever?

But you see, when we walk away from his destiny, we change the plan that God has for our life. Imagine now ... the pages of your book disappearing.

God gave us free will, which allows us the choice to step into His plan—or not. No doubt, you are chosen ... No doubt that He loves you ... No doubt that he is there for you. God is unchanging. He is Jehovah, "I am." Make no mistake ... He has not changed the plot—we have.

So, when we choose God's version of our story, does this mean that life will be perfect and we will all live happily ever after? Does this mean that there will be no more pain and suffering? Do not be misguided by what God's plan is for us. He does not promise us a fairy tale ending in this life. But, when we choose the path He has laid out for us, we know that He is with us, leading and guiding us and that His plans are for good. We also have His assurance that we will spend eternity with Him where he will wipe every tear and welcome us with open arms. Our lives are fleeting, but what we do in this life will determine our destiny for eternity.

So we are convinced that every detail of our lives is continually woven together for good, for we are his lovers who have been called to fulfill his designed purpose. Rom. 8:28 (TPT)

Destiny Chats:

If you could write the story of your life, what would the title be and why?

Outside of major milestones, list three highlights?

Who would be the heroes?
   List at least three and why?

Have you ever won an award or prize?
　What was it, and how did it feel to win?

How does it feel to know you are chosen by God and He has a plan for your life?

Destiny Questions:

Have you chosen the destiny plotted out by God or have you taken a different course?

Why or why not?

Destiny Prayer:

Lord, take my life ... take my story and let it be about what you have done in my life. You are the Master Weaver, intricately weaving every detail of my life together to fit into your perfect plan to bring good into my life. Thank you that you love me and have called me to fulfill your very specific plan purposes through me.
　In Jesus' name, amen.

Destiny Notes:

The Fall

The day Gagglin put himself before his people and regarded them as possessions rather than treasures was the beginning of his departure from his duties. He would pace out about on his perch and call out to the mountains, "Look at this beautiful town I have built! It's the most spectacular land of all! I built this town! Me! This is my town, and these are my people! No one can tell me how to run my empire! No one! I am truly the wisest in all the land!"

His army tried to warn him ... the townspeople pleaded ... the great Council of the Jonakins bid him caution.

"I control it all! These people are beholden to me, only me!"

In Gagglin's obsession with power ... he lost control of himself. No longer did he possess the land—the land possessed him ... and it drove him to madness.

* * *

Gagglin had become so puffed up with himself, he lost control. When you obtain great wealth and power, this is all too easy to do, and sadly, way too common. The book of Daniel tells the same story in the life of King Nebuchadnezzar. In 586 BC, Nebuchadnezzar destroyed the Kingdom of Judah and its capital, Jerusalem. This destruction led to the Babylonian captivity as the city's population and people from the surrounding lands were deported to Babylonia, including Daniel and his comrades. The king was so fearsome, the Jews referred to Nebuchadnezzar as the greatest enemy they had faced until that point, known as a 'destroyer of nations.' The book of Jeremiah describes Nebuchadnezzar as a cruel enemy but also as God's appointed ruler of the world and a divine instrument to punish the disobedience of the children of Israel. Ruling for forty-three years, Nebuchadnezzar held the longest reign of the Chaldean dynasty. At the time of his death, Nebuchadnezzar was among the most powerful rulers in the world. Not knowing God but seeing his power through Daniel, he learned a great lesson in what pride can do. This story is a daunting illustration of how the mighty have fallen, and I hope you take the time to read and study the book of Daniel in its entirety.

But all these things did happen to King Nebuchadnezzar. Twelve months later he was taking a walk on the flat roof of the royal palace in Babylon. As he looked out across the city, he said, 'Look at this great city of Babylon! By my own mighty power, I have built this beautiful city as my royal residence to display my majestic splendor.'

While these words were still in his mouth, a voice called down from heaven, 'O King Nebuchadnezzar, this message is for you! You are no longer ruler of this kingdom. You will be driven from human society. You will live in the fields with the wild animals, and you will eat grass like a cow. Seven periods of time will pass while you live this way, until you learn that the Most High rules over the kingdoms of the world and gives them to anyone he chooses.'

That same hour the judgment was fulfilled, and Nebuchadnezzar was driven from human society. He ate grass like a cow, and he was drenched with the dew of heaven. He lived this way until his hair was as long as eagles' feathers and his nails were like birds' claws.

Daniel 4:28 -33 (NLT)

All the worldly status we achieve will go away in the end.

Don't store up treasures here on earth, where moths eat them and rust destroys them, and where thieves break in and steal. Store your treasures in heaven, where moths and rust cannot destroy, and thieves do not break in and steal. Wherever

your treasure is, there the desires of your heart will also be. Matthew 6:19-21 (NLT)
Johnny Cash sang a haunting song called "Hurt", originally written and performed by Trent Reznor of the band Nine Inch Nails. Some of the most profound lines in the song state, *"Everyone I know goes away in the end. And you can have it all. My empire of dirt."* The depth of the lyrics is beyond riveting ....

Destiny Chats:

Who are some of the most powerful people in the world today?

Would you say they have achieved success by godly means?

Where has this success brought them, and what is the fruit of their success?

What are some of the successes that you have achieved in life that you are most proud of?

What is the secret to your success?

Have you been able to use your position to build up God's kingdom?

Destiny Questions:

Our heart is our treasury, and it will reveal our innermost thoughts.

A good person produces good things from the treasury of a good heart, and an evil person produces evil things from the treasury of an evil heart. What you say flows from what is in your heart. Luke 6:45 (NLT)

Where is your treasure?

Is your answer reflected in your life and actions?

Destiny Prayer:

Lord, take it all. It's all yours anyway. I release all that I have to you. You are the Giver. You are my Provider. You are my Treasure.
   In Jesus' name, amen.

Destiny Notes:

Blood

You are not forgotten, for you have been chosen and destined by Father God.
The Holy Spirit has set you apart to be God's holy ones, obedient followers of Jesus
Christ who have been gloriously sprinkled with his blood.
May God's delightful grace and peace cascade over you many times over!
I Peter 1:2 (TPT)

"Blood for blood!" I said to the boys, "When I give you the blood of Lavir, he will make the ultimate sacrifice by giving his Awakening for the slumber of Zephyr. His blood will defeat the vile Zephyr and keep him from rousing for a thousand years. In turn, Lavir will not arise for the Great Awakening. It is what he wants. As he has done before, he will do again ... lay down his Awakening for those whom he loves."

* * *

The Band of Brothers needed the blood of Lavir to defeat the evil Zephyr. In doing so, Lavir laid down his Awakening, not knowing if the mission would be successful or not. This wild analogy draws an illustration of what Christ did for us.

You see, no matter how hard we try, we cannot achieve righteousness, on our own, and God hates sin. We are fallen individuals in need of a Savior. God longs for perfect unity with us, and because of this, He made a way for all of us to come to him by receiving the sacrifice of his only son, Jesus. The Creator actually died for the created. Just think about this for a minute.

As fallen humans, we are not capable of living a sinless life, no matter how hard we try. That's why we absolutely needed the Lamb who was slain to take away our sins. You see, before Jesus came to earth, the Jews would sacrifice a lamb as an atonement for the sins of the Jewish people. This was a foretelling of Jesus' ultimate sacrifice. Jesus was the only Lamb who was worthy to take on our sins because he had no sin. He was the spotless Lamb. His blood was shed to cover our sins. When we invite Jesus into our lives, we are washed in His blood, and God's anger is pacified because of this covering.

Once we receive the sacrifice of Jesus, by becoming his child, we are then entered into His destiny.

The Father has an intense love for me because I freely give my own life—to raise it up again. John 10:17 (TPT)

Jesus laying down his life for us was only the first part of the story. The second part of the story is that as Jesus raised his life up again, he will also raise our life up in Him. Whatever hardship you have been through or life you have had before Christ is covered by His blood. Now, the next best part comes—your new relationship in Jesus where He beckons us to fulfill the Prophecy.

There is an old Christian hymn called "There's Power in the Blood". As a child, I never really thought about the meaning of the lyrics but just sang along. Now, as an adult, I understand the lyrics and know that without the blood of Christ, we would not have our salvation. The blood of Jesus is what separates Christianity from other religions. Jesus did not ask us to die. Instead, He died for us and He became the sacrifice. This was His destiny, and he took this on because He loves us.

I surrender my own life, and no one has the power to take my life from me. I have the authority to lay it down and the power to take it back again. This is the destiny my Father has set before me. John 10:18 (TPT)

Jesus' God-given destiny was to be the sacrifice to take away sins, and now he is our mercy seat because of his death on the cross. We come to Him for mercy, for

God has made a provision for us to be forgiven by faith in the sacred blood of Jesus.
Romans 3:25a (TPT)

Destiny Chats:

Are you a perfectionist? If so, can you share how being a perfectionist has worked out for you?

Have you ever given up something you really loved, whether it be an item, activity, or relationship? How did it feel?

Can you think of a kind act someone has done for you?

What do you think motivated this person to act in such a way?

Some think that by being a good person, they can work their way to heaven. How would you respond to this?

Why do you think Jesus went to such great lengths to make a way for our salvation?

Have you ever asked Jesus to come into your heart? If so, can you share your story?

They conquered him completely through the blood of the Lamb and the powerful word of his testimony. They triumphed because they did not love and cling to their own lives, even when faced with death. Revelation 12:11 (TPT)

Destiny Questions:

Have you been gloriously sprinkled with Christ's blood? If not, there is a prayer in the back of this book under the "Destiny Awaits" section that will help walk you through this step of faith. Now is the time to invite God into your destiny and break Satan's curse for you.

If you are a Christian, have you invited Jesus into your destiny? Being a Christian is more than a prayer. It is a daily walk. What areas in your life are keeping you from fulfilling God's plan for you?

Destiny Prayer:

Lord,

Thank you for your glorious blood that was shed for me when you made the ultimate sacrifice with your life. Your blood—and your blood alone—paved the way for me to enter into the destiny that you have laid out just for my life! All my works are as filthy rags, and I can never thank you enough for laying down your life for me. May I walk in obedience as I follow your calling.

I love you!

In Jesus's name, amen.

Destiny Notes:

Sacred Gifts

It is the same Holy Spirit who continues to distribute many
different varieties of gifts. The Lord Yahweh is one,
and he is the one who apportions to believers
different varieties of ministries. The same God distributes
different kinds of miracles that accomplish
different results through each believer's gift and ministry as he energizes
and activates them. Each believer is given continuous revelation
by the Holy Spirit to benefit not just himself but all.
I Cor 12:4-7 (TPT)

The young, noble warriors overwhelmed my very being ... Now, the time had come for final instructions and the presentation of the sacred gifts.

As the Band of Brothers stood before me, I looked each of them directly in the eye. I had no doubt that these fine young men were more than conquerors, but even conquerors can fall ... so I gave them a final caution. "I am sending you out, like sheep among wolves. You are to be wise and cautious. You will encounter danger and peril at every turn, so you must be alert. Your enemies will prowl like lions, seeking to devour you, but stay the course—one step at a time. Do not sway to the right or the left. It is imperative to stay focused ... as you never know when they will strike. Darkness awaits you at every turn. Although I cannot be with you in a physical presence, I entrust each of you with a sacred token from the order of the Jonakins. These items are assigned to you for this mission exclusively."

* * *

The power of unity is overwhelming, and when we make Christ the center, we are truly unstoppable. Each of the Band of Brothers had unique gifts that were exclusive to them, given by Exijah. They relied on the strength of each other's gifts to help break the strongholds in order to fulfill the mission. In much the same way, the Lord gives us our unique gifting to build one another up in Christ so that we may fulfill our mission on earth.

By using our gifts together, we are able to see the power of God and the true miracles that He wants to reveal to us. These miracles are essential to our walk with Christ, and He is the one who activates and energizes them. Through this, we are given divine revelation to benefit not just ourselves, but others.

Walking in our gifting is essential to reaching our destiny. If you think you do not have gifts from God, you are mistaken. You can always ask God to reveal to you what gifts you have. You see, just like a parent, God loves to give gifts to his kids.

God has given each of you a gift from his great variety of spiritual gifts. Use them well to serve one another. I Peter 4:10 (NLT)

Destiny Chats:

What is the first present you can remember?

What are some of your favorite gifts that you have received?

What are a few meaningful gifts that you have given or received?

To the best of your knowledge, what sacred gifts do you possess?

How are you using these gifts to help others?

Destiny Question:

How about taking a spiritual gifts test? You can record your answers in this section. This can help you better understand the many gifts that God has given you as you move forward in your destiny of empowering not just yourself but others.

https://www.alfredstreet.org/wp-content/uploads/2019/05/ASBC-Spiritual-Gifts-Survey.pdf

After taking the spiritual test, record your top three gifts here, and in notes, comment on how you can incorporate these gifts into your life.

Destiny Prayer:

Thank you Lord, for the unique gifts that you gave just to me. May I grow in this gifting and use it to build up your body as I grow in my walk with you. Please activate all you have for me in my life, that I may be energized in you and bring blessings and miracles that come from you in my daily walk.

In Jesus' name, amen.

Destiny Notes:

Shame Game

Their one ceremony of the year was in honor of the greatest shamer, known as the Master Winchinist. "He who shames is he who saves," they chanted as the Mayor placed the despicable trophy in their hands. The "Great Wall of Shame" was reserved as a display for those who were the greatest shamers of all.

* * *

We live in a shaming society where the shaming never ends. It's easy to point fingers but as you will read in *Awakening of the Giants* when you point one finger, four fingers point back at you or maybe five ... if you're a giant.

Whatever road you have traveled on, there have no doubt been bumps. In some cases, you may have made the right choice and in other cases, you may have chosen poorly. That's what being human is all about. We are imperfect beings in need of God's mercy. God is so gracious with his mercy and is begging us to come to him in spite of our failures. All we need to do is receive his forgiveness.

By giving ground to shame, not only are you harming yourself but you are in danger of passing it on to others. This is our human nature and it's easy to allow shame to fester in our soul and make ourselves feel better by pointing out others' faults. So no matter how hard we work to cover shame, it will eventually rear its ugly head.

For all that is secret will eventually be brought into the open, and everything that is concealed will be brought to light and made known to all. Luke 8:17 (NLT)

If you have an area that is hidden in darkness, this is a breeding ground for shame. By asking God to shine his light on this hidden area in your life, you will break the power of sin that wants to ravage your very being. Don't let Satan use this sin against you. Break its power by confessing your sin to God and turning away.

The next step is moving on to forgive yourself. Sometimes it seems we are hardest on ourselves. If God can forgive us, why can't we forgive ourselves and others?

Just like the Band of Brothers, we are called to break the shame, not just in our lives but in others. Shame tells us that we are guilty and deficient. Jesus tells us that we are guiltless and free as his grace covers our weaknesses. Christ already paid the price for our sins. As we trust Jesus for forgiveness and as our provider, shame will lose its power over us. No need to play the "Shame Game". Shame is defeated through the redeeming work of Jesus. As we receive this gift, we will never wear that shame-face again.

Destiny Chats:

Why do you think shaming is so prevalent in our society?

Have you experienced being shamed in your own life?
   How did you react?

No doubt you have witnessed someone being shamed at the hand of a shamer?
   What happened and how did you respond?

Death on the cross was the ultimate shaming game and Jesus took this punishment for us. Throughout his life, he was continually challenged for standing for truth. As we stand firm in our faith, we can be assured the same will happen to us.
   What are some strategies that Jesus used, when shamed by others that we could apply to our own lives?

In this divided world that we live in, what strategies have you used to avoid falling into the shame game?

Do you wear a shame-face? If so, why?

Destiny Questions:

Now is your time to break free. Is there a sin that is holding you from your destiny?

As you confess this sin to Christ, are you able to experience his forgiveness and remove the shame-face?

Destiny Prayer:

James 5:16a (NLT) encourages us to, *"Confess your sins to each other and pray for each other so that you may be healed."*

If you feel the need to confess this sin to someone, your Band is designed to be a safe place, and now is the time for healing.

Lord,

Search my heart and see if there be any wicked way in me and lead me in Your way everlasting. I confess that I am a sinner, saved by grace. Thank you that your grace is sufficient and covers all. Thank you that those who look to you are radiant and their faces are never covered with shame.

I love you!

In Jesus' name, amen.

Destiny Notes:

Faith

Faith shows the reality of what we hope for;
it is the evidence of things we cannot see.
Through their faith, the people in days of old earned a good reputation.
And it is impossible to please God without faith.
Anyone who wants to come to him must believe that God exists and
that he rewards those who sincerely seek him.
Hebrews 11:1, 2, 6 (NLT)

"Yes, this is a perilous situation, indeed. The giants are awakening, and the river currents are the epicenter of force."

"How will we ever cross?" Jerzam desperately pleaded.

"I will give you my suggestions, but ultimately it depends on each of you working together. This mission requires faith. As I said earlier, focus on what is ahead."

"That's the most frightening part, what lays straight ahead—and above." Jerzam wanted to be hopeful, but the situation at hand appeared dismal indeed, and they were only just beginning.

"You are called to fulfill this Prophecy, so all you can do is step into your destiny."

"Agreed," the brothers chimed.

"Listen and listen close. You are all going to count to three and then throw the gravel that you just put in your pocket towards the river—After that, run directly into the path that you have thrown."

"Wait ... you mean, like, into the river?" Zed looked confused and discouraged.

"You will know where to turn as the gravel will direct you. Step out in faith," I instructed them.

"If we go into that river—we'll drown." Neko dismayed.

"Or get eaten..." Zed was aghast.

"The choice is yours—but I suggest you step out."

* * *

As they faced death, the Band of Brothers had to decide quickly whether to move forward in faith or shrink back in fear. Sound familiar?

Life is filled with little and big decisions every day. Many decisions you soon forget, but even little decisions can have lasting consequences. Making big decisions is never easy, especially when under pressure with no time to consider the ramifications. Making a big decision can be paralyzing to some and indecisiveness can lead to the feeling of being stuck. The art of making a decision is one of the greatest tools you can add to your arsenal.

However, faith is the essence of any decision, in spite of who or what you have faith in. Whether you believe in God or not, you must have faith because you are not all-seeing and all-knowing. Perhaps your decision-making method of faith is called "luck" or "common sense" or "fate", but whatever it looks like, your decisions affect your destiny.

If we had all the answers, we would have no need for faith. But since we are finite humans with free will, God has provided us with a lifeline to Him through Jesus. Yes, that's right! God the Creator of the universe, who is all-seeing, all-knowing, and all-powerful, offers us his guiding hand to steer us through our journey. What could be better?

It's the difference between flying a plane on autopilot or having Jesus as your copilot. I am so thankful that I have known Jesus since my youth. The biggest decisions of my life have been steered by Christ and I cannot imagine the consequences of not having Him at the wheel. The sooner you invite Jesus to be your copilot the better.

Jesus even invites us to ask Him for wisdom, and He will freely give it without holding it against us.

And if anyone longs to be wise, ask God for wisdom and he will give it! He won't see your lack of wisdom as an opportunity to scold you over your failures but he will overwhelm your failures with his generous grace. James 1:5 (TPT)

Whether you are a believer or not, you have the capability to make good decisions and poor decisions. I certainly have made my share of bad decisions. However, whatever the case, Jesus is there for us. Perhaps you are a follower of Christ and you have not yet invited Jesus into your decision-making process? Maybe you have never understood how easy it is and worthwhile? It's never too late to start inviting God into every decision of your life. God is a generous God who loves to bless His children. In fact, as His image-bearers, did you know we have his mind?

For, "Who can know the Lord's thoughts? Who knows enough to teach him?" But we understand these things, for we have the mind of Christ. I Cor. 2:16 (NLT)

Destiny Chats:

Here are some of the top big decisions:

- Become a follower of Christ (or not)
- Start a new job/position (or not)
- Get married (or not)
- Start or end a relationship (or not)
- Pursue a degree (or not)
- Have/adopt a child (or not)
- Get a pet (or not)
- Buy a home (or not)

- Quit a job/position (or not)
- Move to a new state (or not)
- Choose where to study/what to study [2]
- Devote time or effort to academics/ sports/ hobby (or not)

From the above list, can you pick the top three decisions that made the biggest impact on your life? How did you arrive at these decisions? What was the outcome?

What are the little, daily decisions that impact your life greatly?

Share a time when you were in an unsure situation and you had no idea what to do?

Can you explain what happened and how you handled it?

Where do you turn when you have a tough decision to make?

Are you seeing a pattern in your decision-making? Please describe?

Destiny Questions:

In retrospect, what advice would you give to your younger self if you had to make these decisions again?

Moving forward, how will you apply what you have learned from your past decisions to your future decisions?

Destiny Prayer:

Dear Jesus,

Thank you that you are all-present and all-knowing, that I can come to you for wisdom and that you will freely give it. I invite you into my decision-making, no matter how big or how small. I ask you for wisdom, that I may walk into the destiny that you have set before me. Thank you that you love to bless your children. I love you.

In Jesus' name, amen.

Destiny Notes:

Destiny Notes to my children/young person:

The Crossing

Set your gaze on the path before you.
With fixed purpose, looking straight ahead, ignore life's distractions.
Proverbs 4:25 (TPT)

I mmediately, billowing clouds of smoke and enormous pillars of fire blazed into the air and raced down the river. The dragon's laser-focus eyes spotted the chaos that ensued and headed directly towards the disturbance at lightning speed. The Band of Brothers had to decide quickly whether to charge into the blazing river while the dragons stormed their way or retreat into the forest to be hunted down like wild animals. They froze in confusion as they pondered their impending doom.

Then, they remembered my words: "Run directly into the path you've thrown." Jerzam stepped out first ... next Figgles—Moklee, Zed, and Neko knew better than to get separated again, and they followed suit, not knowing where the path would take them or if they would meet their fate.

* * *

The rewards of faith are overwhelming. Faith is what we cannot see but what we hope for. As discussed in the last chapter, it wouldn't be faith if we knew what would happen next. Sadly, life often brings us to a crossing, and we are

surrounded by dragons and predators that would like nothing more than to see us fail. Making a good decision is just the first step—once we walk into our destiny, we are only just getting started. Now, more than ever, is the time to stay the course and run into the path we have thrown.

But how do we do that when we are surrounded by chaos and mayhem? Temptation is always lurking, and we know that Satan's goal is to steer us off our course. The whispers in our ears to turn to the right and the left can be overwhelming, and once headed in the right direction, it is not very difficult to lose our way.

In Matthew 14, we learn about Jesus walking on water. His disciples were terrified until they realized that the person walking on the water was Jesus. Peter insisted on joining Jesus and was doing just fine until he looked at the raging waves around him and began to sink. What a great portrayal of how easy it is to focus on the storms around us and take our eyes off God. Jesus reached and grabbed Peter and said, *"You have so little faith. Why did you doubt me?" Matthew 14: 31 (NLT)*

Making the right decision is truly the first step, but staying the course is taken one step at a time as we keep our eyes on Christ. Like the tree planted in the water, we are not moved when the rains and storms come.

The very essence of life can truly be more dramatic than what see in *Awakening of the Giants* because it's real life. Walking in shame and condemnation will only paralyze us more. Our God, who loves us, is filled with grace. Not only will He provide you with the strength to stay the course as we come to Him, but He will forgive us when we go astray and lovingly pursue us to bring us back. God is our biggest cheerleader!

The Son of Man has come to give life to all who are lost. Think of it this way: If a man owns a hundred sheep and one lamb wanders away and is lost, won't he leave the ninety-nine grazing the hillside and thoroughly search for the one lost lamb? And if he finds his lost lamb, he rejoices over it, more than over the ninety-nine that never went astray. Now you should understand that it is never the desire of your heavenly Father that a single one of these little ones should be lost.
Matthew 18:11-14 (TPT)

Destiny Chats:

If you could have dinner with one famous person, dead or alive, who would it be and why? (Not including Jesus because he is always with you)

What qualities did/does this person possess that you most admire?

Are you a boater? If so, can you share about one of your favorite boating adventures?

Life is a highway, and I'm gonna follow all night long ....
    Tell us about one of your favorite road trips and what you loved about it?

Are you a road warrior with no stops but straight ahead, or do you like to veer off course and explore new places?

Would you say you are a single-focused person who is all-in or more impulsive and non-committal?

Are you a sports fan? If so, who is your favorite team and why?

Fave player and what you love about him/her?

Do you currently compete in a sport, or perhaps you did at one time? If so, what sport was it, and what did your training look like?

Did your team ever win an award? If so, why or why not?

What lessons did you learn from this activity? What was the reward for your hard work and perseverance?

Destiny Questions:

Is Jesus aboard your boat? Do you see a common thread that has led to success or not?

What does it look like for you to stay the course to cross into your destiny?

Destiny Prayer:

Lord,

I invite you to be the captain of my boat. I am just a passenger, and I desperately need you to steer the course of my life. Please help me fix my eyes on you and not be swayed by the storms of life that come my way. You alone are my rock and my refuge. In you, I trust.

In Jesus' name, amen.

Destiny Notes:

Spiritual Warfare

Put on salvation as your helmet, and take the sword of the Spirit,
which is the word of God.
Ephesians 6:17 (NLT)

"**W**ritten hundreds of years ago by the Jonakins and preserved by the Hulus, these Scrolls contain the virtues of the Jonakins, recorded to help and guide others in their life journey. Right here, in our underground, we have possession of the Scrolls of Balwik."

"Wow! Really?" Figgles looked amazed.

"Seriously?" Zed appeared as if he struck gold, and indeed he had.

"This carving tells us that the answer to breaking the strongholds is in the Scrolls, which is why we study daily so that we can be prepared."

* * *

In the beginning the Word already existed. The Word was with God, and the Word was God. He existed in the beginning with God. God created everything through him, and nothing was created except through him. The Word gave life to everything that was created, and his life brought light to everyone. The light shines in the darkness, and the darkness can never extinguish it.

John 1:1-5 (NLT)

So the Word became human and made his home among us. He was full of unfailing love and faithfulness. John 1:14a (NLT)

We live in a fallen world, and we have an enemy.

Be well balanced and always alert, because your enemy, the devil, roams around incessantly, like a roaring lion looking for its prey to devour. I Peter 5:8 (TPT)

Note that, I Peter 5:8 refers to Satan as "your" enemy, and make no mistake, he is "your" enemy indeed. Every day is a new frontier as we are attacked on all sides, and if we are not prepared for the battle, we will get devoured. Satan is a lying, cunning deceiver, who will stop at nothing to bring about our destruction. The sad reality is his job is all too easy. He simply applies the same old schemes he has used since the Garden of Eden and the sheep come running to the slaughter.

When the Bible was written, the sword was essential for battle. What soldier would go to war without being prepared? If we are to win this fight, we must equip ourselves. Ephesians 6:10-20 clearly outlines the weapons of our warfare, but for this *Destiny Awaits Devo*, we are going to dive into the Sword.

John 1 tells us that the Word of God is Jesus. Jesus is the Word. He existed in the beginning and he became human and made his home among us. Ephesians 6:17 tells us that the sword of the Spirit is the Word of God. When we take up our sword, we are activating the very Creator of the universe to fight our battles. God gave us the key to the universe and the ultimate weapon of protection in His word—and it is living.

Have you ever considered how incredible the Word of God is? The Word is the Bible, and it is one hundred percent written by man and one hundred percent inspired by God. Written on three different continents, in three different languages by forty different men from all walks of life over a span of fifteen hundred years yet resounding in perfect harmony. Over three hundred prophecies were fulfilled in Christ's life and death alone and his prophecies are still being fulfilled today.

The Bible has far surpassed the test of time and is the greatest historical record. Just to give you an idea of the scarcity of other historical records and the abundance of Biblical records, here's a brief list.

```
Plato — 7 copies
Caesar — 10 copies
Euripides - 9 copies
Aristotle — 49 copies
Homer's Illiad - 643 copies
More than 5,300 known Greek manuscripts of the New Testament.
```

The uniqueness of the Bible comes not only in its historical accuracy and incredible consistency but in the guarantee of eternal life that is a free gift when we come to Jesus. The old saying "You may be the only Bible others read" bears repeating. When you are living and breathing the Word of God, you are a living testimony. Not only will your life change but the lives of those you encounter will feel the power as you shine the light of His Word. You see, the Word gave life and light to everyone, and it is so intense that the darkness can never extinguish it. Why not apply this power daily to our arsenal?

God gave us this manual to know Him better and also to fight off the enemy. By reading God's Word and living his Word, we are absorbing the very essence of Christ as He steers our destiny.

When Satan hurls insults and attacks your way or casts lies in your head, you can take up the sword to fend off his attacks. The most powerful warriors in ancient days were master swordsmen. Likewise, in order to win our daily fight, we must master our weapons.

The power of memorizing and applying the Scriptures to your life is so incredible, it can actually rewire your brain. The Word of God has the power to help you overcome negative thought patterns and destructive behavior. By allowing God's word to sink into your very soul, your life will be transformed.

So let's try it ....

Here's a great verse for you. Say it or read it three times and wait to see what happens in your soul and then, write it down.

And I am convinced that nothing can ever separate us from God's love. Neither death nor life, neither angels nor demons, neither our fears for today nor our worries about tomorrow—not even the powers of hell can separate us from God's love. No power in the sky above or in the earth below—indeed, nothing in all creation will ever be able to separate us from the love of God that is revealed in Christ Jesus our Lord.

   Romans 8:38 & 39 (NLT)

Destiny Chats:

How did this passage speak to you?

What three words in this passage stand out to you and how do they apply to your life?

It's so easy to take the Word of God for granted and forget that God left this love letter for us because He loves us so much more than we can ever imagine. Nothing can separate us from his love, so why not reach out to him through His Word?

His Word gives us discernment to identify truth from lies.

   Just for fun, if you are in a group, let's play two truths and a lie. You can think about it for a minute and then write down two truths and one lie in the lines below. The other members of your group will have to figure out which statement is not true.

Truth

Truth

Lie

What is your definition of truth?

How did you decipher the truth from a lie in the above game? How do you decipher truth from a lie in life?

What do you believe the basis for truth is?

The definition I love for truth was given to me by my philosophy prof and it states, "A statement that is true states what is and what is not. A statement that is false, states what is not is and what is, is not." That seems simple enough ... yet in this day and age, truth has become very twisted, so it is more important than ever to know the difference between a truth and a lie.

Have you ever been scammed by a hoax? What happened and how did you get taken?

What did you learn from this process?

Have you ever served in the military or know someone who has served?

What tactics would you or your friend/family member say, are key to winning a battle?

Destiny Questions:

As a soldier serving in the army of God, are you equipped with your sword to fight the battle? If not, what needs to happen to take up your sword daily and have it permeate your very soul?

Destiny Prayer:

Lord,

Thank you for your Word. Thank you that you are the Word. Thank you that you came to make your home among us through the Holy Spirit and your Living Word. May I live and breathe your Word, so I can stand strong against all that comes my way.

In Jesus' name, amen.

Destiny Notes:

The Power of Encouragement

I am contending for you that your hearts will be wrapped in the comfort of heaven and woven together into love's fabric. This will give you access to all the riches of God as you experience the revelation of God's great mystery—Christ.

Col 2:2 (TPT)

"Jerzam, I want you to understand that the power of your Anakalite blood lies in your ability to lead and encourage others. Not by strength or sacred gifts, but by truly working together as a team, you will conquer. As we discussed, but it bears repeating, as you bring out the best virtues in each of your Band of Brothers, you will fulfill the Anakalite blood that flows in your veins and find the light that comes from within. Let this ring be a reminder to you of who you are and your calling."

* * *

So I'm asking you, my friends, that you be joined together in perfect unity—with one heart, one passion, and united in one love. Walk together with one harmonious purpose and you will fill my heart with unbounded joy. Phil. 2:2 (TPT)

I don't think the Word of God could be any clearer when it comes to the power of encouragement. God's manual to us is the ultimate guide to encouragement. It offers every encouragement for life and living to fill our hearts. Like medicine, the word of God brings healing to a wounded soul.

Encouragement can provide people with the strength to look ahead, move forward, and reach for the next goal. Your whole life can be transformed through encouragement. Even when the going gets tough, encouragement makes your outlook look brighter. Some people are extravagant with encouragement, but no one can outperform God's encouragement.

Look at how much encouragement you've found in your relationship with the Anointed One! You are filled to overflowing with his comforting love. You have experienced a deepening friendship with the Holy Spirit and have felt his tender affection and mercy. Phil. 2:1 (TPT)

You see, encouragement stems from our relationship with Christ. As our faith deepens with the Holy Spirit, we become like him, and His encouragement to us overflows and we can't help but overflow his love to others. As Christians, we are the aroma of life to those who are perishing. But did you know that even our presence can bring life and light?

... but believers smell the life-giving aroma that leads to abundant life. And who of us can rise to this challenge? 2 Corinthians 2:16b (TPT)

It's easy to fall into seclusion and focus so much on our "to-do" list that we forget about others. The good news is that encouragement doesn't have to take a long time. It can start with just a smile. A smile translates into any language. How about telling those closest to us "I love you!" I can't tell you how many people have told me that their parents never told them that they loved them when they were children. How hard is it to tell those nearest and dearest to us that we love them? Even if it doesn't come naturally, can you move a bit out of your comfort zone to share His love? Ask the Lord for strength to build on your encouragement and see where it goes. Grow as you go! Beware—you may become an extravagant encourager.

Never underestimate the power of telling someone you love them. Tell your spouse. Tell your children. Tell your friends. If you have time for a note, send it their way. Love begins at home, and it is the basis for a healthy family. Healthy families are the basis for a healthy world. Love makes the world go around. So let's love, and love big! Encouragement is love.

The power of encouragement will not only bless others but will fill your soul. It will bring about unity, and with unity comes strength. You will be a light shining bright for all to see. Others will know you by your love.

Destiny Chats:

If you already are a person of encouragement, please share how encouragement has changed an otherwise dark situation in your life or someone else's
life?

Can you think of a recent encouraging statement you made to someone and
how it changed their outlook?

Now reverse the previous question. Can you share a time when you received
an encouraging word and how it changed your outlook?

I'm sure we can all remember when someone gave a discouraging word. So
why is it that we remember the discouraging words so much more than the
encouraging words?

Are you an eternal optimist, or do you prefer to think of yourself as a cynical
pessimist or somewhere in-between?

Can you define what has attributed to your state of optimism or pessimism?

What are a few ways you could offer additional encouragement to those closest to you?

Have you ever offered an extravagant expression of encouragement to a stranger?
Can you share how it affected you and the other person?

How profound is the power of encouragement? Can you share your thoughts?

Now, it's time to share encouragement from your heart with the person on your right. When finished, take a minute to write down that encouragement in your "Destiny Notes."
Another option would be to pass your journal to the person on your right and let them write out their encouragement to you below.

Destiny Questions:

Are your closest relationships encouraging or discouraging? If they are not encouraging, what part can you play in changing this situation? On the other hand, perhaps you have relationships keeping you from your destiny?

Also, time for self-reflection. Are you an encourager? Would those closest to you agree with this assessment? If not, why not, and how can you become one?

Destiny Prayer:

Lord,

Please help me to see others through your eyes of love. Would you take off my half-empty glasses and put on your half-full glasses? I want Jesus' spectrum lenses so that I can focus on the good in life and bring your encouragement everywhere I go. Thank you for your grace in my life and may I be able to extend that grace to others.

In Jesus' name, amen. 3

Destiny Notes:

Breaking Strongholds

Day two... Broke the stronghold of Krindel and took down the Laughing Giant with laughter! Despair is crushed, and hope has been restored! Day three, we head to Winchin to break down shame and anything that gets in our way.
Destined to overcome!
Figgles.

For although we live in the natural realm, we don't wage a military campaign employing human weapons, using manipulation to achieve our aims. Instead, our spiritual weapons are energized with divine power to effectively dismantle the defenses behind which people hide. We can demolish every deceptive fantasy that opposes God and break through every arrogant attitude that is raised up in defiance of the true knowledge of God. We capture, like prisoners of war, every thought and insist that it bow in obedience to the Anointed One. Since we are armed with such dynamic weaponry, we stand ready to punish any trace of rebellion, as soon as you choose complete obedience. 2 Corinthians 10:3–6 (TPT)*

* * *

We live in a spiritual world, and we are soldiers under God's command. If our eyes were opened, we would see the cataclysmic fight between the forces of good and evil waging war against us, much like Goggen and Gagglin's mission against their kingdom.

When I was a child, tracts were very common. These were little booklets that shared how to become a Christian and often had comic illustrations. The drawings of the demons luring Christians to fall into the trap of sin were the pictures that stood out to me. Although these illustrations seemed a bit hokey, in reality, they accurately portrayed Satan's mission against our very lives and souls quite well. Satan is armed and dangerous. As a soldier in God's army, I caution you not to dismiss the ever-present darkness that we battle every day.

When the Lord showed us how to pray ....

Lead us not into temptation but deliver us from the evil one. Matt. 6:13 (NIV)

We know from Scripture that when Jesus was on earth, He was tempted in every way.

He understands humanity, for as a man, our magnificent King-Priest was tempted in every way just as we are, and conquered sin. Heb. 4:15 (TPT)

When Satan tempted Jesus in the wilderness, he offered him all the kingdoms of the world and the splendor that came with it.

But Jesus said, "Go away, Satan! For the Scriptures say: Kneel before the Lord your God and worship only him." Matthew 4: 10 (TPT)

Jesus used the Word of God as His arsenal.

Jesus was attacked on every side, but He overcame. He stood against hunger after not eating for forty days. *Can we call this the temptation of comfort?*

He withstood demonstrating his powers as the son of God by not taking Satan out, before the appointed hour.

Perhaps we would understand this as our timing versus God's timing?

Then, ultimately, he resisted the "cosmos", the world and its system, being handed to him by Satan.

We might look to this as the temptation of pride and power?

Are not all of these temptations common to our everyday life? This verse pretty much sums it up.

For everything in the world—the lust of the flesh, the lust of the eyes, and the pride of life—comes not from the Father but from the world. I John 2:16 (NIV)

So how then shall we live? We are riddled with temptation and often we fail? As fallen beings, how can we withstand the many battles to reach the destiny the Lord has for us?

The definition of a stronghold in the Bible is a fortified place, a place of refuge and protection.

The Lord is a refuge for the oppressed, a stronghold in times of trouble. Psalms 9:9 (NIV)

The Lord wants to be our stronghold, but when we allow the lusts of the flesh and the pride of life to take the place of God's provision, we find ourselves bound in a false sense of security that does not lead to our destiny but rather, to our demise.

As we give in to temptation, we choose Satan's plan over God's plan. We take comfort in the things of this world and not the provisions of God. Just like when the Band of Brothers broke the strongholds of the giants, we are called to break the strongholds in our hearts that are taking the place of God. God, and God alone, is our refuge and strength. There is never a situation out of God's control, so the best place to be is right with Him.

The character of God is a tower of strength, for the lovers of God delight to run into his heart and be exalted on high. Proverbs 18:10 (TPT)

Isn't it comforting to know that we can run into the heart of God as our stronghold?

Destiny Chats:

As a child, did you have a secret place that you would run and hide in?
  What made it special?

66

Do you have a place that you run to now to escape?
Perhaps a favorite getaway?

When you are under stress, what activity provides you with a reprieve from the chaos?

Let's take a closer look at the strongholds identified in 2 Corinthians 10:3-6. First, we are called to *"dismantle the defenses that people hide behind."*
What could these defenses be? Can you think of a few common defenses that you or others hide behind, and how you dismantle them?

We can *demolish every deceptive fantasy that opposes God.* Fantasies, thoughts, or imaginations can be strongholds.
Can you name a few examples of what a deceptive fantasy, thought, or imagination could be in your life or others? How would we demolish these pretenses?

We can *break through every arrogant attitude that is raised up in defiance of the true knowledge of God.* What does this look like in everyday life? Can you list an example of breaking an arrogant attitude that raised itself against God?

We capture, like prisoners of war, every thought and insist that it bow in obedience to the Anointed One. What are some thoughts that need to be captured? How do we make them obedient to God?

We stand ready to punish any trace of rebellion, as soon as we choose complete obedience.

Are there areas of rebellion in your life that need to come under the obedience of Christ?

Destiny Questions:

If you have answered these questions honestly, you have just identified strongholds in your life that need to be broken. By the divine power of God and the spiritual weapons that you have been given in Ephesians. 6, you can effectively demolish these strongholds that have built up in your life.

Take a moment for some personal inventory and make a list of the strongholds that need to be broken. Can you invite God to take the place of these false fortresses?

Have you chosen complete obedience as mentioned in 2 Cor. 10:6b?

Destiny Prayer:

Thank you, Lord, that you have armed me with such dynamic weaponry. Thank you that you are my strong tower and fortress, an ever-present help in times of trouble. May I walk in complete obedience, that I may energize your divine power in my life to dismantle the defenses of darkness as I pursue the destiny that you have for me.

In Jesus' name, amen.

Destiny Notes:

Power of Destiny

The light shines in the darkness,

and the darkness can never extinguish it.

John 1:5 (NLT)

T he power of destiny rang even louder than the echoing of the cracking earth as it weaved its way up to Gagglin's perch—the light was shining on the darkness.

* * *

Can you not discern this new day of destiny breaking forth around you?

The early signs of my purposes and plans are bursting forth.

The budding vines of new life are now blooming everywhere.

The fragrance of their flowers whispers, "There is change in the air."

Arise, my love, my beautiful companion, and run with me to the higher place.

For now, is the time to arise and come away with me.

Song of Songs 2:13 (TPT)

The power of destiny is waiting to burst forth in your life. God wants to be your GPS and take you on an adventure so big and so amazing, you will rise up out of the ground. All ready to jump aboard? Now is the time ....

As the power of destiny rips through your heart and soul, others will see it, and your very being will bring life and light so bright that the darkness will not be able to extinguish it. You will glow in the dark, just like Jerzam!

We have become the unmistakable aroma of the victory of the Anointed One to God—a perfume of life to those being saved and the odor of death to those who are perishing.

2 Cor. 2:15 (TPT)

Though the enemy will continually attempt to set you off course, we have the weapons of our warfare that enable us to stand, stand, stand ... against the enemy's tactics.

We may take a U-turn here and there or look to the right or the left, but even then, our God awaits for us as He will leave the ninety-nine for the one. Our God, who loves us as his dear children, will not turn you away when you get back on track.

The Son of Man has come to give life to all who are lost. Think of it this way: If a man owns a hundred sheep and one lamb wanders away and is lost, won't he leave the ninety-nine grazing the hillside and thoroughly search for the one lost lamb? And if he finds his lost lamb, he rejoices over it, more than over the ninety-nine that never went astray. Now you should understand that it is never the desire of your heavenly Father that a single one of these little ones should be lost. Matthew 18:11-14 (TPT)

Have you taken a U-turn? It's never too late to come back to the fold. God is not just waiting for you but longing for you to return home, with open arms. Whether you have ventured a little or a lot, God is there for you ... longing to take you on the journey that was designed especially for you. Do not allow Satan to take you off course any longer. Now is the time to allow God's sweet breath to flow through your veins, empowering you with his life and light for you to pursue all that He has for you.

Destiny Chats:

Share a time when you were lost? Where were you and what happened?
How did you find your way back?

If you are a parent, have you ever lost your child or left your child behind?
What happened, and how did you find your child?
Otherwise, if you were that child who was lost, we would love to hear about it.

What did it feel like to be lost or to have lost someone you loved?

Destiny is the road map that the Lord has for us, but sometimes it means change.
Are you a person who struggles with change and takes comfort in the familiar, or do you long for adventure and love change?

If you are currently on course to your destiny, can you share some life-altering adventures that brought you to where you are? This is your testimony of what God has done in your life.

God never stops working to draw us to Him. What are some recent God sightings that you have seen in your life?

Destiny Questions:

God is our Waymaker, who is making the way just for you! He is calling you to step into the destiny that He has planned for you. If you have not done this yet, what is holding you back?

If you are walking in your God-given destiny, take a moment to thank the Lord for where he has brought you.

Destiny Prayer:

Dear Jesus,

Whom shall I fear? If you are for me, who can be against me? You are my Waymaker, Miracle Worker, Light in the darkness. Thank you for leading and guiding my path and going after me when I go astray. Thank you for always being there for me.

In Jesus' name, amen.

For those who have not surrendered your life to Christ, now is the time to invite him into your destiny.

I invite you to say this prayer.

Jesus,

Will you take my GPS and be my anchor? I want you at the wheel, not myself. I want all that you have for me. I want Christ alone, the only way to my destiny. I invite you to take over my life and cover me with your precious blood that you shed for me on the cross.

I ask you to forgive me for taking my life into my own hands.

I acknowledge that you are Lord of all.

I acknowledge you as my Lord and Savior.

I invite you into my heart, and I run into your heart that overflows with love and forgiveness.

I love you, Jesus!

If you said this prayer for the first time, you have just invited Jesus into your heart and chosen Him as the Lord of your life. You are on your way to the destiny that He has for you

Do you not feel it? Do you not perceive?

The power of destiny sweeping through your heart?

Destiny Notes:

Date I invited Jesus into my heart:

The Challenger

The Lord is close to the brokenhearted;
he rescues those whose spirits are crushed.
Psalm 34:18 (NLT)

"Day after day, hour after hour—they lived under the fear of Mushkin. Those that dared to stand up to him ... failed miserably. There was no way to stop the 'Stomping Giant'—the name given to him by the villagers. They felt defeated, so defeated, and to add insult to injury, the Mayor referred to them as 'The Losers!'"

"How dreadful!" Jerzam couldn't be any more distraught.

"Not being able to overcome the defiance and strength of the Stomping Giant, they gave up. To this day, they live under this label. They walk with their shoulders slumped and their heads hung low. They are a defeated people with heavy hearts."

* * *

The Book of Psalms is filled with references to the enemy. As a child, I used to wonder, "Who is my enemy?" Perhaps some of you may wonder the same today? But, sadly, the beautiful innocence of childhood comes to an end when you realize that the world is filled with enemies. The Bible has many names for our enemies, "Satan," "the world," "the flesh," and anything that stands against the truth of God.

Sadly, most of us are all too familiar with the "Challenger." These are those who like nothing more than to bring others down. These are the people who think they know it all and work to undermine the abilities of those around them. No matter how we respond to these individuals, we will never be correct, and even if we were, they dare not hear us. Satan uses these individuals to harass us and bring us down. It's much easier to walk away from these individuals altogether, but sometimes, they are our family members, co-workers, neighbors, and supposed friends. So, how do we respond?

The reality is, we are all broken people and we are not at a loss for opportunities to hurt others and likewise be hurt. We have all been a part of this vicious cycle. If we have been hurt by someone, no doubt we have hurt others.

The first step to resolving a broken relationship is to own up to our part in the mishap. We are called to walk in humility and love. It's easy to point fingers, but when we ask God to search our hearts to see if there be any wickedness, we can come clean. Pursuing your destiny is all about the willingness to allow God to search our hearts and clean up anything that is hindering the path He has paved for us.

Just as God forgave us, we need to forgive others. This doesn't mean we have to continue in an unhealthy relationship, it just means that we have to walk in humility and repentance. If you have likewise offended this person, whether it be the "Challenger" or anyone for that matter, then, by all means, take ownership and do not just apologize, ask for forgiveness.

Likewise, if someone has offended you, Matthew 18:15-19 gives us very clear instructions on how to restore broken relationships. We are called to go that person directly and if they do not repent, bring a witness.

"Truly I tell you, whatever you bind on earth will be bound in heaven, and whatever you loose on earth will be loosed in heaven." Matthew 18:18 (NIV)

Both the power of forgiveness and unforgiveness have ripple effects that reach all the way to heaven. This is why a broken relationship has such power over our hearts and soul. Unless we are able to walk in humility and make this relationship right before God and man, we will be walking in defeat, and Satan will use this as a stronghold in our life to keep us from all that God has for us.

Wherever you are in your journey, the Lord is near to you and crying out for you to come to him with your hurts. Whatever part is up to you, he is calling you to lay it at his feet and make it right.

Beloved, don't be obsessed with taking revenge but leave that to God's righteous justice. For the Scriptures say: "Vengeance is mine, and I will repay," says the Lord. And: If your enemy is hungry, buy him lunch! Win him over with kindness. For your surprising generosity will awaken his conscience, and God will reward you with favor. Never let evil defeat you, but defeat evil with good. Romans 12:19-21 (TPT)

Nothing can stand against the power of our God, even our enemies. They may still want nothing more to do with you for whatever reason they contrive. You may need to take a step back from this person for your own self-protection, but our job is done when we do all we can to live at peace, and then we are able to give it to God. You see, as a child of God, the battle belongs to Him!

Then, we can walk with our heads and shoulders held high, our spirits soaring and our hearts at peace, knowing we have done our part. Then, we hear the sounds of freedom that rise all the way to heaven. This is what freedom looks like.

So no wonder we don't give up. For even though our outer person gradually wears out, our inner being is renewed every single day. We view our slight, short-lived troubles in the light of eternity. We see our difficulties as the substance that produces for us an eternal, weighty glory far beyond all comparison, because we don't focus our attention on what is seen but on what is unseen. For what is seen is temporary, but the unseen realm is eternal.

2 Corinthians 4:16-18 (TPT)

Destiny Chats:

Have you recently had a disagreement with someone close to you?
    Was this situation resolved, and how could you have avoided this conflict?

Let's be real, what kind of fighter are you?
    Passive-aggressive? You bottle it up and then one day, explode?
    Just plain aggressive? Don't mess with me or I'll let you have it?
    Just plain passive? I don't know and I don't care? Perhaps I deserved to be mistreated?
    No nonsense? Let's cut to the chase!

Is your current method working?
    Why or why not?

Have you ever had someone vent their anger on you for no apparent reason?
    How did you resolve it?

What methods of conflict resolution have you found to be the most effective?
    Are you utilizing them?

Have you had to break off unhealthy relationships in your life?

What warning signs were there, telling you to run?

Can you share an example of a restored relationship in your life that was brought about through godly principles?

Destiny Question:

Is there a "Challenger" in your life that has created issues that need to be addressed? If so, what is the first step to resolution (as much as is up to you)?

Destiny Prayer:

Thank you, Lord, that you never give up on us. Thank you for comforting us when we hurt and forgiving us when we fail. Search my heart "oh Lord" and see if there be anything that needs cleaning up. Free me from holding on to any offense that I'm holding onto and likewise, I set that person free in Christ Jesus. I lay it at your cross. All I have and all I am is yours.

In Jesus' name, amen.

Destiny Notes:

When I had nothing, desperate and defeated,
    I cried out to the Lord and he heard me,
    bringing his miracle-deliverance when I needed it most.
The angel of Yahweh stooped down to listen as I prayed,
    encircling me, empowering me, and showing me how to escape.
    He will do this for everyone who fears God.
Psalm 34:6&7 (TPT)

Stand Strong

But whether I live or die is not important,
for I don't esteem my life as indispensable.
It's more important for me to fulfill my destiny
and to finish the ministry my Lord Jesus has assigned to me,
which is to faithfully preach the wonderful news of God's grace.
Acts 20:24 (TPT)

N ow in the dark cavern, Jerzam's glowing body lit up the atmosphere. The boys endured the dragon frisk as each giant creature made its rounds.

"Are we going to die?" asked Moklee.

"Perhaps they're deciding which of us to eat first?" Neko proposed.

"We will not die! Together, we'll fight!" Jerzam declared as the menacing-looking beasts glared at them with fire in their eyes. With each declaration, Jerzam's body burned brighter.

"Puff! Snort!" the dragons snarled, now looking more threatening than ever.

Jerzam knew the peril they were in, but he was not about to let the Band of Brothers become their next meal. "We stand strong by order of Exijah, to fulfill the Prophecy that foretold our arrival!" Now, his body was so bright ... the dragons had to squint their yellow eyes.

In times of peril, it only seems natural to be at a loss for where to turn.

Ephesians 6 is quoted often in this guide but now let's take a look at verses 11 & 13 in the NIV.

*Put on the full armor of God, so that you can take your **stand** against the devil's schemes.*

*Therefore put on the full armor of God, so that when the day of evil comes, you may be able to **stand** your ground, and after you have done everything, to **stand**.*

Stand! Stand! Stand! Do you hear a common theme here? Satan wants to take us off course and do all he can, to knock us to the ground and seize us like prey.

Stay alert! Watch out for your great enemy, the devil. He prowls around like a roaring lion, looking for someone to devour. I Peter 5:8 (NLT)

Lions are known for hiding at a distance so that they can stalk their prey by watching their every move. Then suddenly, they pounce and capture their unsuspecting prey by breaking their neck with their powerful jaws as they slowly suffocate the life out of their victim. How close does this sound to the enemy's tactics for us? As we **stand** strong with our feet firmly planted and suited for battle, we will be prepared for when the day of evil comes.

Not only are we to **stand**—but we are to **stand** strong! The Greek word for strong is a combination of the word *en*, which is a preposition meaning in, by, or with, and *dunamoo*, a form of *dunamis*. *Dunamis* means to be filled with inherent, active, achieving power. Because we're strong "in the Lord," it's the same kind of power He has. We are to **stand** with the *dunamis* power given to us in Jesus Christ. We have authority in Christ when we **stand** in Him, and, much like the Band of Brothers said to the dragons, "You will not take us down!" We can likewise **stand** firm knowing that the power that has raised God from the dead is the power that we are **standing** in when we invite Jesus into our destiny.

Indeed, life is filled with many trials, temptations, and tribulations, but as we **stand** strong in the *dunamis* power given to us in Christ Jesus, we will be like that tree planted in the water.

But blessed are those who trust in the Lord and have made the Lord their hope and confidence. They are like trees planted along a riverbank, with roots that reach deep into the water. Such trees are not bothered by the heat or worried by long months of drought. Their leaves stay green, and they never stop producing fruit. Jeremiah 17:7&8 (NLT)

I don't think I could explain it any better than Psalm 46 (TPT).

God, you're such a safe and powerful place to find refuge. You're a proven help in time of trouble—more than enough and always available whenever I need you. So we will never fear even if every structure of support were to crumble away. We will not fear even when the earth quakes and shakes, moving mountains and casting them into the sea. For the raging roar of stormy winds and crashing waves cannot erode our faith in you.

Pause in his presence.

God has a constantly flowing river whose sparkling streams bring joy and delight to his people. His river flows right through the city of God Most High, into his holy dwelling places. God is in the midst of his city, secure and never shaken. At daybreak his help will be seen with the appearing of the dawn. When the nations are in uproar with their tottering kingdoms, God simply raises his voice, and the earth begins to disintegrate before him. Here he comes! The Commander! The mighty Lord of Angel Armies is on our side! The God of Jacob fights for us!

Pause in his presence

Everyone look! Come and see the breathtaking wonders of our God. For he brings both ruin and revival. He's the one who makes conflicts end throughout the earth, breaking and burning every weapon of war. Surrender your anxiety. Be still and realize that I am God. I am God above all the nations, and I am exalted throughout the whole earth. Here he stands! The Commander! The mighty Lord of Angel Armies is on our side! The God of Jacob fights for us!

We have a God who fights for us! As we **stand** in his power, our Commander and the mighty Lord of Angel Armies is on our side! We are not fighting alone!

Can you take a pause and acknowledge that the Creator of the Universe fights for you?

Let's **stand** up and give God a standing ovation! He is worthy!

Destiny Chats:

What is God telling you through Psalm 46?

When you were a child, or maybe you are a child, what fears did you have? Were or are, they rational or irrational?

Do you still have these fears? As you look back, now, can you see how Jesus intervened?

Can you share a time when you were in peril, and you saw God's mighty hand deliver you?

Psalm 46:10 tells us to "Surrender your anxiety." What does this look like in your life?

What's the opposite of not surrendering your anxiety?

Destiny Questions:

Are there any areas in your life right now where your knees are quivering?
What do you need to do to stand strong?

Now, take a pause and picture Jesus, the Commander, the mighty Lord of
Angel Armies, standing alongside you? What do you sense now?

Destiny Prayer:

*Lord, you are my strength and my refuge. Would you please take my weak knees
and strengthen them? Straighten my back that I might **stand** strong with your
dunamis power. If there is an area where I am faltering, I surrender it to you.
In Jesus' Name, amen.*

Destiny Notes:

.

Living Water

*Then on the most important day of the feast, the last day,
Jesus stood and shouted out to the crowds—"All you thirsty ones,
come to me! Come to me and drink!
Believe in me so that rivers of living water will burst out from within you,
flowing from your innermost being, just like the Scripture says!"*
John 7:37-38 (TPT)

"They're shooting up everywhere!" Figgles flapped his wings in delight, trying to soak it all in.

"They must be the ancient wells breaking free. Goggen has not seen clean water in hundreds of years. The cracking of the earth has released them," the Queen explained.

"Now it's streaming through the streets!" Figgles was so excited he nearly flew away.

"The Mushkinites will be delighted to see fresh, clean water. They have only heard of the wells through the Tales of Tamin."

"Look! They're jumping in it! That looks like so much fun!"

"They are being cleansed by streams of living water. They were dead, but now they're alive," Queen Welda said. "The Scrolls of Balwik describe the 'Fountain of Life' that cleanses and heals."

* * *

The Mushkinites had not had fresh water for hundreds of years. The erupting streams brought about new life and birth to a town that was decimated and destroyed. How closely does this sound to places you may have visited, whether physically or spiritually? Darkness is all around us, and when you enter a zone without light, it is evident.

The reality of not having clean water is all too real in third-world countries. Having fresh water is a blessing that we all too readily forget to appreciate. However, if we ever go without water, we soon realize the fragility of our very existence.

I experienced the lack of fresh water on a mission trip that I took to a third-world country. In this impoverished area, clean water was delivered on a truck. The homes in the area had a cistern underground, and the water trucks would fill up the tanks for families to have water for bathing, cleaning, and even flushing the toilet. Sadly, these were the more established homes in the remote neighborhoods. I shudder to think how the poorer homes accessed freshwater, but what I do know is the only water that was safe for drinking was bottled. To us, who are accustomed to simply turning on the faucet and jumping in the shower, this seems all too foreign.

Water is the source of life. Without water, we would cease to exist. When Jesus proclaimed to be the living water, he could not have made his message any more straightforward. John 7:37b-38 (NIV), listed above, tells us that Jesus actually stood up at one of the main Jewish festivals and shouted in a loud voice.

Let anyone who is thirsty come to me and drink. Whoever believes in me, as Scripture has said, rivers of living water will flow from within them. John 7:39 (NIV)

Jesus was making a bold statement, in the boldest way, to the very people who were seeking to kill him. Why would he do such a thing?

So, what exactly is this living water that Jesus shouted about so resolutely?

By this, he meant the Spirit, whom those who believed in him were later to receive. Up to that time the Spirit had not been given, since Jesus had not yet been glorified. John 7:39 (NIV)

Jesus was referring to the Holy Spirit that flows through us after we invite

Jesus into our hearts. His Spirit is the very embodiment of God, and this is a personal invitation to us to partake of this power. This is why the New Testament repeatedly tells us to be filled with the Spirit. When we are filled with the Spirit, we are a river of life to all around us, overflowing Jesus.

You see, we live in a barren land that is quickly turning away from God with hardened hearts and seared souls. They are thirsty, but they do not know where to turn to be quenched, so they turn to cheap substitutes hoping to be satiated. Those filled with the Spirit are living water to the very being of the parched and dehydrated sojourner looking to find their way. We draw this living water when we go to the Well, which, in turn, overflows from within.

In Acts 2, the Holy Spirit comes upon the believers for the first time, and they are filled with power. The living water was so overflowing that the locals thought they were drunk!

In Acts 2:17-19 (TPT), Peter stands up with the eleven disciples to explain what was going on.

This is what I will do in the last days—I will pour out my Spirit on everybody and cause your sons and daughters to prophesy, and your young men will see visions, and your old men will experience dreams from God. The Holy Spirit will come upon all my servants, men and women alike, and they will prophesy. I will reveal startling signs and wonders in the sky above and mighty miracles on the earth below. Blood and fire and pillars of clouds will appear.

When we are overflowing with the Living Water, others will notice, and your atmosphere will be transformed by the mighty power of the Holy Spirit activated in you. Some around you will be repelled, and others will be drawn to the Christ in you. This is God's plan for us and why Jesus was so excited! He was the water delivery man coming to a third-world land saying, "I am here! I have the most incredible gift for you! All you have to do is come to me and be filled!"

Many are still drinking from the old, contaminated water that brings death and destruction. They are lost in the desert, searching for the source of life, but they do not know where to find it. When the river of life flows onto them, the desert blooms, and dry bones come to life.

Is anyone thirsty? Come and drink— even if you have no money! Come, take your choice of wine or milk— it's all free! Isaiah 55:1 (NLT)

Jesus answered, "If you drink from Jacob's well, you'll be thirsty again, but if anyone drinks the living water I give them, they will never be thirsty again. For when you drink the water I give you, it becomes a gushing fountain of the Holy Spirit, flooding you with endless life!"

John 4:13-14 (TPT)

Holy Spirit, come!

Destiny Chats:

Have you ever been to a third-world country and experienced no running water?

How was water distributed?

Did you get sick from drinking contaminated water or perhaps food that had been contaminated by the water?

Can you describe a time when you entered a place, and you felt darkness? Where was it, and can you describe the scenario?

Jesus faced ongoing insults and persecution for proclaiming truth while on earth, have you ever experienced this? Can you explain?

Walking filled in the power of the Holy Spirit is something every believer in Christ is called to do, yet it is easy to get bogged down in life, and our hearts become dry and weary.

Do you know someone who is overflowing with the river of life? What are they like?

Is that person you?

Can you describe a time when you entered a dark setting, and the river of life inside of you brought life and light?

Destiny Questions:

Are you thirsting for living water and leaking Holy Spirit?

What steps do you need to take to be flowing with rivers of life?

If overflowing, keep going!

Destiny Prayer:

Lord, may the river of life flow through me so that everywhere I go, I spread life and love—less of me and more of you, Jesus. You are my river! You are my source! You are my hope! Come, Holy Spirit! Come, fill me up to overflowing, that I may walk and move in your power.

In Jesus' name, amen.

Destiny Notes:

And He also said, "It is finished! I am the Alpha and the
Omega--the Beginning and the End. To all who are thirsty I will
give freely from the springs of the water of life."
Rev. 21:6 (NLT)

Banded Together

"You are 'Overcomers!'
You are a Band of Brothers with a bond that cannot be broken!"

Two people are better off than one, for they can help each other succeed. If one person falls, the other can reach out and help. But someone who falls alone is in real trouble. Likewise, two people lying close together can keep each other warm. But how can one be warm alone?
A person standing alone can be attacked and defeated, but two can stand back-to-back and conquer. Three are even better, for a triple-braided cord is not easily broken.
Ecclesiastes 4:9-12 (NLT)

* * *

God gave us each other because we need one another. Unfortunately, loneliness is very prevalent in our world today. Often it comes from protecting ourselves from hurt and then not allowing others into our lives, and suddenly, we wonder why we are all alone.

It's good to have some moments of solace to pray and reflect, but when we isolate ourselves completely, we have moved into an unhealthy place that God did not intend for us. After God created Adam, he said, *"It is not good for man to be alone. I will make him a helper who is just right for him." Genesis 2:18 (NIV)*

The Band of Brothers had each other as lifelong friends. Filled with virtue and strength of character they stood faithfully by each other's side, offering encouragement and support in the midst of ongoing hardships.

There are "friends" who destroy each other, but a real friend sticks closer than a brother." Proverbs 18:24 (NLT)

For purposes of this *Devo*, we are calling the friends who stick closer than a brother, your "Band".

Having a Band is a gift from God. Perhaps your Band is one person, or you are blessed to have several members in your Band? Maybe your Band is a childhood friend? A co-worker? A neighbor? Or even your brother, sister, mother, or father? If you are married, hopefully, your spouse is your number one Band.

The Bible offers very clear guidelines on what your Band should look like:

· Your Band should bring life. *As iron sharpens iron, so a friend sharpens a friend. Proverbs 27:17 (NLT)*
· Your Band should love you well. *Love each other with genuine affection, and take delight in honoring each other. Rom 12:10 (NLT)*
· Your Band should help you up when you are down. *If one person falls, the other can reach out and help. But someone who falls alone is in real trouble. Ecclesiastes 4:10 (NLT)*

The Bible also offers very clear guidelines on what your Band should not look like:

· If you are closest to those who have ungodly character, it's time to reevaluate.
  Don't be fooled by those who say such things, for "bad company corrupts good character." I Cor. 15:33 (NLT)
· If your Band is gossipy and divisive, you can be sure you will have division and drama. *A troublemaker plants seeds of strife; A gossip separates the best*

of friends. Proverbs 16:28 (NLT)

· We are cautioned to avoid relationships with individuals who are quick to anger or we could become just like them. *Don't befriend angry people or associate with hot-tempered people, or you will learn to be like them and endanger your soul. Proverbs 22:24 & 25 (NLT)*

Are we looking for perfect individuals to be in our Band? Well, we know we are not perfect so we will be very lonely if we wait for a Band without flaws.

Therefore, as God's chosen people, holy and dearly loved, clothe yourselves with compassion, kindness, humility, gentleness, and patience. Bear with each other and forgive one another if any of you has a grievance against someone. Forgive as the Lord forgave you. And over all these virtues put on love, which binds them all together in perfect unity. Col. 3:12-14 (NIV)

If you are looking for your Band of Brothers or Sisters, you can be sure the above ingredients will bind you together in love.

Destiny Chats:

Speaking of bands, have you ever been in a "musical band"? If so, tell us more.

Who is your favorite musical artist/band? Favorite song?

Have you ever connected with someone who didn't seem like your usual Band, but then you became closer than a brother/sister?

What qualities are important to you with those who you call your Band?
Are these qualities evident in your Band?

Do you have a Band of Brothers/Sisters?
Tell us about them?

Can you share a significant time when your Band came together in a time of need?

We all go through seasons in life. Perhaps you had a Band at one time but no longer do.
If not, what happened, and do you think it's important to get the Band back together?
Perhaps the Band will look different now?

If you do not have a Band, what steps do you think you need to take to find your Band?

If you have a Band, what do you love most about them?
What role do you play in offering them a safe and life-giving environment?

Destiny Question:

Examine your closest friendships? Are they clothed in compassion, kindness, humility, gentleness, and patience? Are you bound together in love, walking in unity? If so, that's awesome. If not, is it time to take a closer look?

Destiny Prayer:

Lord, thank you for giving us one another. Thank you for the gift of friendship. May you lead and guide my relationships in compassion, kindness, humility, gentleness, and patience. Please forgive me for my shortcomings and how I treat others and give me the strength to bear with others as they have faltered. May you bind our hearts together in love as we walk in unity to build your kingdom.

In Jesus' name, amen.

Destiny Notes:

Freedom

"The Spirit of the Lord is upon me, and he has anointed me
to be hope for the poor, healing for the brokenhearted,
and new eyes for the blind, and to preach to prisoners,
'You are set free!' I have come to share the message of Jubilee,
for the time of God's great acceptance has begun."
Luke 4:18&19 (TPT)

A s the Hope Dust took its effect, the villagers began to look straight ahead and suddenly realized what was going on.

"We are no longer prisoners!" one said.

"No turning back!"

"Let my people go! Let my people go!"

Now that the townspeople grasped the gravity of what almost happened to them, they all joined in.

"Let my people go!" they chanted.

* * *

Can you hear the sound of freedom ripping through the streets of Goggen as the Band of Brothers fulfill their mission? Strongholds are being broken! Chains are falling off! Hearts are being set free!

What does freedom look like in the Bible? Isaiah 61:1b (NLT) shares a very significant prophecy that was foretold around 700 years before it would come to be fulfilled.

He has sent me to comfort the brokenhearted and to proclaim that captives will be released and prisoners will be freed.

How astonishing that God allowed us this insight into the mission of the Messiah that only He could fulfill through his sacrifice on the cross. He was the Chosen indeed.

This begs the question, "Who are the captives?" When I was in college, I was invited to partake in a prison ministry held at Cook County Jail. I had never visited a prison and had no idea what to expect as a young, naive college student, but I agreed to go. Upon arrival, I had more than one reason to be taken back. Cells with prisoners lined the hallway that we walked down to get to the meeting room. Upon arrival, I realized that I was the only female, surrounded by male prisoners, a few male volunteers, and the Chaplain. As if that wasn't overwhelming enough, I was then informed I would be giving a sermon.

The Chaplain seated our team in the front of the room facing the prisoners. As we took turns sharing the words the Lord had given us, the prisoners passionately responded with heartfelt "amens" and raised their hands to give glory to God. The Holy Spirit covered our room like falling Hope Dust. I was astonished! How were these prisoners so filled with freedom even amid their incarceration?

When my turn came, I had no idea what I would say, and having no time to prepare, I quickly and silently asked the Lord for a word. And then the moment arrived. I stood before this large group of convicts, still not knowing what would come out of my mouth. Finally, I spoke. "I attend a huge university where I see all kinds of people going about their day, wrapped in chains that bind their hearts. They walk in defeat, with their shoulders slumped, and it is evident that they are being held captive. Yet, I come here today and see that the chains in your hearts have been broken. You may be prisoners, but you are freer than many of those I see every day wandering about in their own prison." I closed with, "Who the Lord sets free, is free indeed." I sat down and breathed a sigh of relief when I was done. The prisoners shouted out big hallelujahs, and I could hear freedom ringing from their hearts.

You see, freedom is more than just being able to come and go as we please. *For the Lord is the Spirit, and wherever the Spirit of the Lord is, there is freedom. So all of us who have had that veil removed can see and reflect the glory of the Lord. And the Lord—who is the Spirit—makes us more and more like him as we are changed into his glorious image.*

2 Corinthians 3:17 & 18 (NLT)

Remember what we discussed in the Living Water chapter? We talked about how Living Water is the Spirit that flows inside of us when we come to know Christ. This Spirit of the Lord, inside of us, brings us freedom. If you look at the second part of this verse, the Spirit makes us more like him as we are transformed into the image of Christ. You see, the closer we grow in our walk with Jesus, the more freedom we enjoy, in spite of our circumstances.

Jesus came to set the captives free! Jesus was the Chosen sent to deliver us from the chains brought on by our human condition. When we have a living, breathing relationship with Christ, much like the Band of Brothers, the chains that Satan has bound our hearts with are broken.

Destiny Chats:

2020 was no doubt a challenging year for many around the world. We indeed experienced some loss of our freedoms. What freedoms did you lose that affected you the most?

Were you ever "grounded" as a child? If so, why and what did you do? How did it make you feel?

As you walk around in everyday life, view media, and engage with others, what are some strongholds that seem to be most prevalent? These are the fortresses built up around one's hearts that have them bound in chains.

Do you see yourself struggling with these same strongholds?

Have you ever visited a prison or been in prison/jail?
    Perhaps you know someone who has served time. Describe your experience as you are able.

If you are a believer, can you identify any strongholds that the Lord has broken in your heart?

What did the deliverance of these strongholds mean to your life, and how were you delivered?

Did you hear the sounds of freedom ripping through your own heart?
    Can you share your experience?

Destiny Questions:

What strongholds are holding you back from freedom? Now is the time to be set free. Refer to your Destiny question in chapter 13, and if you have not yet been set free, now is the time to seek God for your deliverance. What would your life be like if you were set free?

But the Lord has paid for the freedom of his servants,
and he will freely pardon those who love him.
He will declare them free and innocent
when they turn to hide themselves in him.
Psalm 34:22 (TPT)

Destiny Prayer:

Lord, thank you for paying the price for my freedom and offering me your grace and forgiveness. In Jesus' name, I break the stronghold of (Fill in the blank), that is binding me and I declare today that I am free and innocent because of the blood you shed on the cross that covered over me when I invited you into my heart. I turn to you, and only you, for my freedom, and I thank you that who the Lord sets free, is free indeed.

In Jesus' name, amen.

Destiny Notes:

Fight for our Lives!

"We will not die! We fight for our lives!" proclaimed Figgles.

"We fight for the Olaquins!" declared Moklee.

"We fight for the Goggenites!" added Zed.

"I do not doubt that you will fight. On the contrary, I stand firm that you will succeed. Nevertheless, know this—the two greatest evils you are about to face will do everything in their power to destroy not just you ... but all of us. That is all for now."

* * *

The battle rages, and here are the headlines ....
Life Versus Death?
Good Versus Evil?
Light Versus Darkness?
The Tree of Life or the Tree of Death?
The Prophecy Versus the Curse?

You have been invited to the fight of the millennium times ten! Who are the

106

contenders? It's YOU versus Satan, and he's brought all his demons to bring you down. You are surrounded. Everywhere you turn there is darkness. Evil lurks from corner to corner. Even in your mind and your very soul, you are being tempted to take a wrong turn. "Don't look straight!" the demons shout in your head. "Look to the left! Look to the right! It's much more exciting. Think of the pleasure it will bring you. What joy you will have if you just bite from that fruit … That beautiful fruit that just hangs there waiting to be eaten." Satan watches in lustful zeal as the trap is set before you. The demons rub their hands together and salivate, waiting for any misstep. They would like nothing more than for you to stumble and fall.

"There you go. Once you eat from the tree you will be so much happier. Your eyes will be opened. You will be like God." The demonic forces sizzle in anticipation as you move towards the bright, shiny, succulent trap set before you. As they have done since the days of Adam and Eve, deceiving and alluring, from the most powerful in the land to the weak and defenseless, so they do to you. The battle for your very life! Know this, *the two greatest evils you are about to face will do everything in their power to destroy not just you … but all of us.*

How do we fight this mammoth battle? Do we go for the shiny and bright? Do we think that maybe just a quick bite or sneak peek will suffice? Or do we say, "Satan, get behind me! I am a child in the Lord's army, and I know your tricks, and you aren't taking me down." Indeed we do. We fight for our lives! We fight for the lives of our family! We fight for the lives of those who look up to us as a beacon of light. We stand strong, knowing and declaring, "It may look like I'm surrounded but I'm surrounded by the Lord and his angel armies!"

Satan has been around since the beginning of time, and his wicked schemes and tactics have not changed. Our battle is not just against Satan, but the world—whether it's through the lust of the flesh, the pride of life, or just subtlety as described by C.S. Lewis in *The Screwtape Letters*. "Indeed, the safest road to Hell is the gradual one—the gentle slope, soft underfoot, without sudden turnings, without milestones, without signposts, … Your affectionate uncle, Screwtape." Perhaps his most significant attack on our faith is simply that of indifference?—A distant faith that keeps God at arm's length, preventing us from a living and breathing faith or, truly, any faith at all.

Whatever tactic the enemy uses on us, know this, his end game is really simple, the destruction that leads to our death and, in the end, the fiery flames of hell prepared for Satan and his demons. The fight for our lives is indeed the epic battle and there is none greater. When we invite God, the Creator of the universe, into our hearts and souls, we ask Him to fight for us and, guess what? He wants us to win. Why else would He come to defeat the work of the enemy by defeating Satan at the cross?

So, what does all this mean? If God has determined to stand with us, tell me, who then could ever stand against us? Rom. 8:31 (TPT)

Then Jesus made a public spectacle of all the powers and principalities of darkness, stripping away from them every weapon and all their spiritual authority and power to accuse us. And by the power of the cross, Jesus led them around as prisoners in a procession of triumph. He was not their prisoner; they were his! Colossians 2:15 (TPT)

Jesus won the battle for us! All we have to do is join his army. Feasting on the tree of life sounds a whole lot better than feasting on the tree of death.

To the one who overcomes I will give access to feast on the
fruit of the Tree of Life that is found in the paradise of God.
Revelation 2:7b (TPT)

Destiny Chats:

Have you ever been trapped? If so, how did you escape?

Describe a time when you felt you were in peril?
  What happened and how did you find safety?

Have you ever had a near brush with death?
  What happened and how were you rescued?

Have you ever rescued someone else's life?

How real do you feel the battle against the enemy is?

Do you believe that the fight against Satan is our greatest battle?
  Why or why not?

How do you fight your battle against the enemy?
  How do you overcome it?

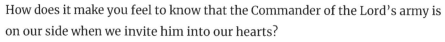

How does it make you feel to know that the Commander of the Lord's army is on our side when we invite him into our hearts?

What picture do you see in your mind?

Destiny Question:

Is there an area of temptation that has seized you that you are having difficulty overcoming? You are more than a conqueror in Christ Jesus. Have you invited Jesus into this battle?

Prayer Response:

Thank you Jesus for fighting for me. I invite you into my heart and ask you to take my battles and to be my Commander in Chief. You are my strength. You are my God. I love you, and I thank you that you love me so much, you died for me, defeating the enemy and making me a conqueror in Christ Jesus!

In Jesus' name, amen.

Destiny Notes:

Hope

Take a decisive stand against him and resist his every attack with strong,
vigorous faith. For you know that your believing brothers
and sisters around the world are experiencing the same kinds of
troubles you endure. And then, after your brief suffering,
the God of all loving grace, who has called you to
share in his eternal glory in Christ, will personally
and powerfully restore you and make you stronger than ever.
Yes, he will set you firmly in place and build you up.
And he has all the power needed to do this—forever!
Amen.
I Peter 5:9-11 (TPT)

"I will, indeed. Remember, there is hope in the darkest places ... and sometimes peace comes from painful things—"

* * *

We have talked a lot about spiritual warfare in this epic devotion that parallels the *Awakening of the Giants* and the fight of evil versus good. At times, we may grow battle-weary, and the fighting can be overwhelming. The idea of escaping and hiding may seem appealing, but where do we go to escape from the swirling chaos that surrounds us? If it is any comfort to your soul, know that we all endure moments of weakness, and we are all in this battle together.

Weeping may last through the night, but joy comes with the morning. Psalm 30:5b (NLT)

The Lord knows how much we can take, and in his great love and compassion, He not only provides us with joy after our sorrow but a reward to those who prevail. Yes, a reward from our all-gracious God who will strengthen your weary bones and make you stronger than ever.

The Sovereign Lord is my strength! He makes me as surefooted as a deer, able to tread upon the heights. Habakkuk 3:19 (NLT)

Your resilience against the enemy will empower and raise you up to shine like a city on a hill shining bright for all to see. No doubt, we will suffer on this earth as we fight for our lives and those around us but know this:

We view our slight, short-lived troubles in the light of eternity. We see our difficulties as the substance that produces for us an eternal, weighty glory far beyond all comparison because we don't focus our attention on what is seen but on what is unseen. For what is seen is temporary, but the unseen realm is eternal. 2 Cor. 4:17&18 (TPT)

When our hearts are troubled, remember that this life is fleeting and that God has prepared a place for us that far outshines anything this world can offer. This is our HOPE—our Hope Dust. What's more, this is our whole destiny. Even though we may travel on some bumpy roads, our eternity with Christ is His plan for us when He will wipe away every tear, and we will see him face to face.

To everyone who is victorious I will let him feast on the hidden manna and give him a shining white stone. And written upon the white stone is inscribed his new name, known only to the one who receives it. Revelation 2:17 (TPT)

So, while living in this "tent," we groan under its burden, not because we want to die but because we want these new bodies. We crave for all that is mortal to be swallowed up by eternal life. And this is no empty hope, for God himself is the one who has prepared us for this wonderful destiny. And to confirm this promise, he has given us the Holy Spirit, like an engagement ring, as a guarantee. 2 Corinthians 5:4-5 (TPT)

We are his betrothed, waiting for our glorious Lord to sweep us off our feet and bring us to his home specially prepared for us. The Holy Spirit—the Comforter—is the guarantee that He is returning and an ever-present reminder that He lives in us. When we grasp the immensity of this reality, we can find hope in the darkest places and peace amid the pain.

Destiny Chats:

If you could sprinkle Hope Dust anywhere, where would it be?

What brings you the most joy and comfort?

Do you remember a time in your life when you felt battle weary?
Maybe that time is now?

Was it hard to see the light at the end of the tunnel?
Can you describe your experience?

What did you learn from this time?

Did you grow stronger or weaker through this time?
Can you share your experience?

Destiny Question:

"Growing stronger every day", is this you? If not, why not, and how do we make this happen? If "yes", what principles are you applying to your life that are working?

Destiny Prayer:

Lord, thank you for being an ever-present help in times of trouble. Thank you for always being there for me. Thank you that you will never leave me or forsake me. You are my hope. You are my rock. You are my salvation. Strengthen my weary bones and help me to focus not on what is seen but what is unseen. I love you!
In Jesus' name, amen.

Destiny Notes:

Chambers

My life, my every moment, my destiny—it's all in your hands.
So I know you can deliver me from those who persecute me relentlessly.
Psalm 31:15 (TPT)

"**W**e did it! We found it!"

"Waaaaaaaaaaaaaaaa!!!!!!!!!!" the boys screamed as they followed close behind Moklee. The wind tunnel felt very much like the entrance to Lavir's heart but with a dark, foreboding presence.

* * *

The Band of Brothers were led to the ultimate test when they headed into the heart of Zephyr. Like lambs to the slaughter, they entered the chambers, not knowing if they would make it out alive. Knowing the plan and the deadly dangers they would face, they did not shrink back. Their families could have held them tight and not allowed them to go, but instead, they released them to fulfill their mission.

When we come to a living relationship with Christ, He calls us to take up His cross and follow Him. The cross is the very symbol of what killed Jesus, yet we are called to carry this symbol as we follow Him.

What if our destiny means we will be persecuted? Why would Jesus lead us into pain and suffering? Why can't the Christian walk be a storybook life where there is no pain and no sorrow? Sadly, we live in a fallen world, which means we are indeed in the war of the worlds. The enemy's attack are especially targeted to Christians—and sometimes, these attacks include being persecuted for our beliefs.

For all who choose to live godly as worshipers of Jesus, the Anointed One, will also experience persecution. 2 Timothy 3:12 (TPT)

Persecution is the hallmark of Christianity. Jesus and most of his disciples died the death of a martyr. Here's just a sample of what awaited the Apostle Paul:

I only know that in every city the Holy Spirit warns me that prison and hardships are facing me. Acts 20:23 (NIV)

```
He is kidnapped (Acts 21:27)
Beaten (Acts 21:30-31; 23:3)
Threatened (Acts 22:22; 27:42)
Arrested many times (Acts 21:33; 22:24; 23:35; 28:16)
Accused in lawsuits (Acts 21:34; 22:30; 24:1-2; 25:2, 7; 28:4)
Stoned (2 Cor. 11:25)
Three times he is beaten with rods (2 Cor. 11:25)
Spent a night and a day in the open sea (2 Cor. 11:25)
Interrogated (Acts 25:24-27)
Ridiculed (Acts 26:24)
Ignored (Acts 27:11)
Shipwrecked (Acts 27:41)
Bitten by a viper (Acts 28:3)
Tradition says that Paul is eventually put to death for his work,
although this is not recounted anywhere in the Bible.
```

Although the persecution we suffer may not bring about bodily harm, it is real and present. Maybe it's the cold shoulder your receive from a family member when you ask if you can bless the meal? Perhaps it's someone at work that knows you're a Christian and calls you a Jesus freak behind your back? What about the classmate who runs the other way when they see you because they know you're the one who doesn't partake in their illustrious behaviors? Whatever it may look like in your life, know that in the end, it comes with a blessing.

How blessed you are when people insult and persecute you and speak all kinds of cruel lies about you because of your love for me! So leap for joy—since your heavenly reward is great. For you are being rejected the same way the prophets were before you. Matthew 5:11-12 (TPT)

Just as Jesus experienced opposition and persecution, we can expect the same. Our reward may not come on earth, but it surely will be ours in heaven. When our hope is in heaven, we can leap for joy knowing that our persecution leads to a greater glory.

Timothy the apostle was sent by Paul to strengthen the persecuted church. Paul warns Timothy:

so that no one would be shaken by these persecutions, for you know that we are destined for this. In fact, when we were with you we forewarned you: "Suffering and persecution is coming." And so it has happened, as you well know. I Thes. 3:3&4 (TPT)

All this begs the question, "Can you live a Christian life without experiencing some level of persecution?" You see, light and darkness are opposite, and when light shines on darkness, the darkness repels. I Timothy promises us that all who live a godly life will be persecuted. If you have not experienced this, perhaps it might be time to ask yourself, "Why not?"

Destiny Chats:

Have you been persecuted for your faith?
  If so, please describe?

If you are a Christian, do you remember before you came to Christ, if you ever persecuted anyone for their faith?

Knowing we will be persecuted, why would anyone sign up to be a Christian?

What does persecution look like for you today?

In the western world, we are free to practice our faith in freedom. However, in many parts of the world, Christians face more than just harassment but risk their very lives. This link will tell you more about the persecuted church. We must remember to pray and help the persecuted church.

https://www.christianitytoday.com/news/2021/january/christian-persecution-2021-countries-open-doors-watch-list.html

Destiny Questions:

After going to the above link, what is the persecuted church experiencing today for practicing their faith?

Am I carrying the cross of Christ? What bold steps is God calling me to take as I live out my faith?

Destiny Prayer:

*Lord, thank you for allowing me the honor of being persecuted for righteousness'
sake. Thank you for the safety and protection you have provided, that I can practice
my faith in freedom. May I be able to appreciate this freedom by boldly proclaiming
that you are Lord and loving loudly. We lift up the persecuted church and pray that
freedom will ring in their lives. My life and my destiny are all in your hands.*

In Jesus' name, amen.

Destiny Notes:

Writing on the Wall

So rejoice, you heavens, and every heavenly being!
But woe to the earth and the sea, for the devil has come down to you
with great fury, because he knows his time is short."
Revelation 12:12 (TPT)

"This wall tells the story of the Curse and how it started ... and how it will end—and now it makes a lot of sense! You see, the first picture shows when I took over Goggen. The giants were subjected to me and did my bidding until ... your dreadful giant, Lavir, came and tried to be a hero, but you see here—he failed! Because this next drawing shows how Lavir died, and the Goggenites fell under the Curse left by the Zamzums' bodies, and how the precious Zephyr Dust enslaves them. Dead or alive—the Curse lives on!"

The boys gasped as they saw a different version of the story depicted on the Hulus wall and my chambers.

"Now, this third drawing shows Zephyr rising and me conquering, not just Goggen but Olaquin—So see, I have a Prophecy too—and it doesn't include you!"

The Band of Brothers were beyond perplexed. This was the opposite of all that had been revealed up to now.

* * *

Have you ever heard the saying, "The writing is on the wall?" This saying refers to a situation that is obviously about to become very difficult. This ancient saying comes from the book of Daniel, chapter 5, when King Belshazzar dared to bring out the gold cups that were raided from the temple of Jerusalem by his predecessor King Nebuchadnezzar. As King Belshazzar and one thousand of his nobles, wives, and concubines were drinking from them, a human hand appeared on the wall and began writing. King Belshazzar was so frightened that his knees knocked in fear, and his legs gave way underneath him.

He called for his astrologers and magicians to translate the writing, but they could not decipher it. Then, his mother informed him of the prophet Daniel who had served Nebuchadnezzar and was known for interpreting dreams and riddles and possessing divine knowledge. So Daniel was brought before the king, and indeed, the writing on the wall was foreboding. Daniel gave a stern warning to the king about his lack of humility and his overt disregard for the Lord by recklessly drinking from the cups of the temple while worshiping false gods. He let him know that, without a doubt, his downfall was coming.

Here's an excerpt from Daniel 5 verses 23b-30 (NLT) that translates the writing on the wall, as Daniel speaks to Belshazzar.

"But you have not honored the God who gives you the breath of life and controls your destiny! So God has sent this hand to write this message.

"This is the message that was written: MENE, MENE, TEKEL, and PARSIN. This is what these words mean: Mene means 'numbered'—God has numbered the days of your reign and has brought it to an end. Tekel means 'weighed'—you have been weighed on the balances and have not measured up.

Parsin means 'divided'—your kingdom has been divided and given to the Medes and Persians."

Then at Belshazzar's command, Daniel was dressed in purple robes, a gold chain was hung around his neck, and he was proclaimed the third highest ruler in the kingdom. That very night Belshazzar, the Babylonian king, was killed. And Darius the Mede took over the kingdom at the age of sixty-two.

King Belshazzar had known about the breakdown of Nebuchadnezzar, but he didn't humble himself before God (We discussed this in Chapter 5), rather, he defiantly dared not to honor God, who is the giver of breath, life, and our very destiny. What a haunting and vivid portrayal Daniel 5 gives of what awaits those who serve themselves rather than God.

See, our enemy, the devil, has already devised the writing on the wall for our lives—much like Gagglin's plans for the Band of Brothers. This plan is a direct assault and attack against not just our lives, but our eternity. Satan is a murderer, liar, thief, accuser, devourer, and every other kind of evil imaginable. Is this who you want to plot out the writing on your wall? But you see, if you have not chosen the Prophecy, by default, you have chosen the Curse.

I recently ran into a young man who had a mighty Biblical name. I said to him, "What a great name!"

He answered, "Yes, it means God remembers."

"How beautiful," I said. "God does remember. I named all my boys after prophets, and they hear God's voice. Do you hear God's voice?"

He responded, "I used to, but I don't anymore."

"What happened?" My heart sunk.

"I chose another plan. I now believe in a philosophy where there is no God, no sin, and no afterlife. This life is all there is."

Sadly, this young man had fallen far from God's plan for his life.

After I shared with Him the love of God and how He is longing for him to return, this young man continued to affirm that he no longer believed in Jesus and even shared that he was a former pastor.

I had to ask, "What if you're wrong? What if you have walked away from the Truth?" His answer was very telling. He said, "Well, then I will have eternity to pay for it."

Again, my heart sank. God is not done with him. I believe our meeting was a divine encounter, and I am praying that God will flood him with believers at every corner. I would covet your prayers for this young man's soul.

Eternity to pay for a bad mistake is a precarious option indeed. This young man rejected the Prophecy and is willing to risk the Curse. Belshazzar refused the Prophecy, and therefore, God spelled it out for him very loud and clear with the writing on the wall.

Walking away from the truth comes in many packages served up by Satan using the same old tricks that he did in the garden.

"Eve, you won't die! Instead, your eyes will be open. You will be like God!"

Satan masquerades his deceitful plan quite creatively. Whether it be through golden cups, a new philosophy, or a beautiful Serpent, the end game is all the same, death, with eternity to pay.

God's unique plan for you is not only specially designed just for you but will fulfill the Prophecy of His story for your life, written on His wall. Here's the difference between the Prophecy and the Curse ....

A thief has only one thing in mind—he wants to steal, slaughter, and destroy. But I have come to give you everything in abundance, more than you expect—life in its fullness until you overflow! John 10:10 (TPT)

I will take abundance, fullness, and overflowing any day over theft, death, and destruction. Our life lived out according to His plan is, indeed, the fulfillment of the Prophecy. It is a quality of life that is designed and directed by the Creator.

We have become his poetry, a re-created people that will fulfill the destiny he has given each of us, for we are joined to Jesus, the Anointed One. Even before we were born, God planned in advance our destiny and the good works we would do to fulfill it! Ephesians 2:10 (TPT)

What a beautiful story to tell. A classic masterpiece awaits!

You see, Jesus came to undo the writing that Satan put on the wall for us ....

But the one who indulges in a sinful life is of the devil, because the devil has been sinning from the beginning. The reason the Son of God was revealed was to undo and destroy the works of the devil. I John 3:8 (TPT)

Destiny Chats:

Why would anyone choose the Curse over the Prophecy?

When you were a child, what did you want to become when you grew up?

Did you fulfill your childhood dream?

If you have grown children, what career did you think they would pursue when they became adults? Were you right?

If you have young children, what do you see as God's plan for them? Be sure to record this in the "Destiny Notes" section.

No matter what age, we all have plans for our lives. What is your plan?

Is there someone you know who has chosen the Curse, and, you have you seen the devastation in their life?

What is the writing on their wall?

Destiny Question:

If you have not chosen the Prophecy yet, you have chosen the Curse. It's time to make a declaration that you are choosing God's plan. If you want to make sure you have invited God into your life, you can head to the "Destiny Awaits" section at the back of this book. Truly, your destiny awaits.

Maybe there's someone in your life who has chosen the Curse. How can you help this person to choose the Prophecy?

Destiny Prayer:

Lord, take my life and my story. May my every breath be controlled by the destiny you have for me. Thank you that you came to undo the works of the devil, and his curse over my life is broken. Would you please lead me to the good works that you would have for me to fulfill? I love you!

In Jesus' name, amen.

Destiny Notes:

The Wicked

Don't follow after the wicked ones or be jealous of their wealth.
Don't think for a moment they're better off than you.
They and their short-lived success
will soon shrivel up and quickly fade away,
like grass clippings in the hot sun.
Keep trusting in the Lord and do what is right in his eyes.
Fix your heart on the promises of God, and you will dwell in the land,
feasting on his faithfulness.
Find your delight and true pleasure in Yahweh,
and he will give you what you desire the most.
Psalm 37:1-4 (TPT)

You had your chance to leave! Say goodbye to yesterday! You chose the Curse—You created this destiny! How did you think it would end? Was it worth it? You've lost everything ... Your town of desolation has left you desolate ... How does it feel?

* * *

The Band of Brothers had come to the end of their mission as they attempted to vanquish Gagglin, and now, they themselves were the vanquished. Their hearts were indeed pure, and they had not veered from the path. Their pure

130

intentions were to free the land of Goggen and protect their land, and now they were the ones imprisoned, confronted by death. How could this happen to them?

Have you ever felt that you have reached the end of your rope with nowhere to turn? You look around, only to see the rest of the world appears to be doing just fine, yet there you are, suffering under a cruel impending doom, awaiting an uncertain future. You cry out, "Why me, God? Look at so and so! They don't even know you and see how great they have it?" Has this ever been your story?

Years ago, I remember an issue with a co-worker whose behavior was way too out of control not to address. As a fellow believer, I followed the guidelines of Matthew 18, where I went directly to this person to attempt to resolve the issue. Since we worked for a Christian company, this seemed to be the best first approach. I asked if we could resolve to put aside our differences in order to work together in unity. I also asked this person if there was any offense on my part that needed to be resolved.

Surprisingly, my co-worker chose to respond with a radical retaliation. I was utterly taken aback, especially since this person was a leader in the Christian community with a big voice. I stressed about the situation and was quite distraught for several weeks. Not only did this person not agree to a plea for peace, but aggressively pursued and threatened my superiors with legal action, calling my attempt, "Religious Harassment". How bizarre, I thought he was a Christian, but perhaps I was wrong?

Not being sure how to react, other than pray, I lamented in my sorrows for a while. "Why me, Lord?" Perhaps I could have handled the situation better, but this was far beyond any conceivable reaction that I had ever experienced.

I turned to the Word of God and found comfort in Psalm 37, as it soothed my wounded soul.

The wicked draw their swords and string their bows to kill the poor and the oppressed, to slaughter those who do right. But their swords will stab their own hearts, and their bows will be broken. Psalm 37:14 & 15 (NLT)

I wondered, "Why would these verses speak to me the most?" I did not wish any harm upon this person. But, sadly, this person had already set their demise in motion. You see, my co-worker chose the Curse over the Prophecy, and darkness over light, as their destiny awaited.

As I prayed and waited for the hand of God to defend me, I searched my own heart. I was instructed by leadership not to communicate with this person lest it rattle their cage even more. When I finally surrendered the situation to God and realized that all my moaning, groaning, and worrying was not going to get me anywhere, I felt free. The chains were broken, and I surrendered my will.

It was just a few months later that the hand of God fulfilled the word He had given me, and did He ever over-deliver. This person was not only released from their high-ranking position but permanently banned from the premises and given a "No Trespassing" warning lest this person attempt to return. As a result, all their status and achievements came tumbling down. The sword this person had used on me had pierced their own heart just as the Psalm said. This individual had worked to defame me, and in the end, was the one who was defamed.

I pray this individual truly was a Christian. Only God knows our hearts, but the actions I perceived were not those of a follower of Christ. As King Nebuchadnezzar and King Belshazzar learned all too well, "Oh, how the mighty have fallen."

God is our defender. God is our judge. When we see the wicked prosper and all the world seems to be theirs, know this, those who trust in the Lord will inherit the land.

Soon the wicked will disappear. Though you look for them, they will be gone. The lowly will possess the land and will live in peace and prosperity. The wicked plot against the godly; they snarl at them in defiance. But the Lord just laughs, for he sees their day of judgment coming. Psalm 37:10-13 (NLT)

Sometimes, even as believers, we choose the Curse and wander in the desert, like the children of Israel. Our stiff necks and stubborn hearts lead us to walk away from the Prophecy, even though we may know it's wrong. Inevitably, we face the consequences of our actions. Thankfully, we are saved by grace or this would be the story for all of us. If you have wandered, our God is waiting for you with open arms to lovingly embrace you when you return to his Promised

Land.

It is comforting to know that when we feel vanquished by our enemies, and feel desperate and weary, God is there for us, and He is our shelter.

The Lord rescues the godly; he is their fortress in times of trouble. The Lord helps them, rescuing them from the wicked. He saves them, and they find shelter in him.

Psalm 37:39 & 40 (NLT)

The key to Psalm 37 lies in verses 5 & 6 (NLT)

Commit everything you do to the Lord. Trust him, and he will help you. He will make your innocence radiate like the dawn, and the justice of your cause will shine like the noonday sun.

Destiny Chats:

What is an enemy?

Have you ever had an enemy plot against you?

Do you know someone very wealthy and flourishing by the world's standards, yet you see their life perishing?

Were you ever in a physical fight as a child?
What started it and what was the outcome?

Have you ever faced an enemy and thought you would be defeated? Can you explain?

What is your greatest comfort in times of trouble?

Have you had a time when you saw God's hand of justice intervene and rescue you?

In reference to Psalm 37:5 & 6, listed above, what does it feel like to have our innocence radiate like the dawn and the justice of our cause shine like the noonday sun?

Destiny Questions:

Is everything you do committed to the Lord? If not, can you trust him to help you in the areas of weakness?
Can you list any areas of your life that are not committed to Him?

Destiny Prayer:

Lord, your ways are not like our ways. We want to vanquish our enemy, yet you call us to love them and forgive them. I pray for anyone in my life who may not have the best intentions for me and may even wish me harm. May you bless them and heal their hearts. May they commit all they do to you that they may shine like the noonday sun. May I live in peace even with those who think of me as their enemies and forgive them as you have forgiven me.

In Jesus' name, amen.

Destiny Notes:

Light

Night's darkness is dissolving away as a new day of destiny dawns.
So we must once and for all strip away what is done in
the shadows of darkness, removing it like filthy clothes.
And once and for all we clothe ourselves with the radiance of light as our weapon.
Romans 13:12 (TPT)

J erzam shone brighter than the morning sun as his body shot out radiant gleams of light that poured over Goggen like the liquid gold of Olaquin, transforming the gray scorched land to verdant green. Streams burst forth in the barren land as budding vines of new life bloomed everywhere, followed by brilliantly colored meadow flowers. The fragrance of the flowers whispered, "There is a change in the air." A sparkling rainbow filled the horizon with the promise of what was to come. The darkness that had overpowered the land for hundreds of years ... was dissolved ... as a new day of destiny dawned.

* * *

It's never too late to invite Jesus into your destiny. He is there for you, even in your final hour. The Light of the world longs for your return to Him. So the sooner you run into his light, the better!

In the beginning, God created the heavens and the earth. The earth was formless and empty, and darkness covered the deep waters. And the Spirit of God was hovering over the surface of the waters. "Then God said, "Let there be light," and there was light. And God saw that the light was good. Then he separated the light from the darkness. God called the light "day" and the darkness "night." And evening passed and morning came, marking the first day. Genesis 1:1–5 (NLT)

On the first day of creation, the first course of action, God said, "Let there be light!" Then he separated the light from the darkness.

Likewise, by radiating his light, we give birth to a new creation in our lives, and our first course of action should be to separate light from darkness as well. Here's an amazing description from the song "Light" by Nathan Wagner.

It's not too late to break the darkness! Father, come down!
Shine! Shine! Shine! Shine your light!
Light! Light! Light!
Oh, shine! Shine! Shine! Shine! Shine your light!
Light! Light!
Let there be! Let there be! Let there be! Let there be!
Let there be light![4]

So don't hide your light! Let it shine brightly before others, so that your commendable works will shine as light upon them, and then they will give their praise to your Father in heaven. Matt. 5:16 (TPT)

As we wrap up our journey in *Destiny Awaits Devo*, I wish you blessings and freedom that you will only find through Christ Jesus. He truly is the only hope to our destiny, and he awaits taking you out of the darkness into the light. May you be filled with purpose for living and breathing as you pursue all that Jesus has for you. May you shine brighter than the morning sun shooting beams of His powerful light everywhere you go, transforming your atmosphere. May your fragrance emanate to all those around you, bringing peace. As Christians, you are Christ's living representation on this earth. You are the light that shines in the darkness.

Indeed, there is change in the air, and it begins in your heart.

The one I love calls to me:

Arise, my dearest. Hurry, my darling. Come away with me! I have come as you have asked to draw you to my heart and lead you out. For now is the time, my beautiful one. The season has changed, the bondage of your barren winter has ended, and the season of hiding is over and gone. The rains have soaked the earth and left it bright with blossoming flowers. The season for singing and pruning the vines has arrived. I hear the cooing of doves in our land, filling the air with songs to awaken you and guide you forth.

Song of Songs 2:10-12 (TPT)

The song Light[5], by Nathan Wagner actually inspired the ending of *Awakening of the Giants* so it seems only fitting to end on this note. The only way to dispel darkness is, indeed, through light. May you be drawn to the light and dispel any darkness that remains in this epic battle of life.

```
Then God said, "Let there be light," and there was light.
Gen. 1:3 (NLT)
```

Hold your breath my love
Just a little bit longer
I am on my way to you
Keep your eyes above
Don't you ever look under
I am gonna rescue you
You see a light's about to break
And every cell is gonna change
Just hold on
Gonna make it through
I know you feel that it's too late
That all these chains have you enslaved
Just hang on
Gonna see the truth
Let there be light

Destiny Challenge:

God, I invite your searching gaze into my heart.
Examine me through and through;
find out everything that may be hidden within me.
Put me to the test and sift through all my anxious cares.
See if there is any path of pain I'm walking on,
and lead me back to your glorious, everlasting way--
the path that brings me back to you. Psalms 139:23 & 24 (TPT)

As your destiny awaits!

Destiny Prayer:

Thank you, Lord, for taking me on this incredible journey. Please strip away all the shadows of darkness in my life and help me to surrender all to you. Clothe me in the radiance of your light.

In Jesus' name, amen.

Destiny Notes:

Destiny Awaits Prayer

Jesus,

Will you take my GPS and be my anchor? I want you at the wheel, not myself. I want all that you have for me. I want Christ alone, the only way to my destiny. I invite you to take over my life and cover me with your precious blood that you shed for me on the cross.

I ask you to forgive me for taking my life into my own hands.

I acknowledge that you are Lord of all.

I acknowledge you as my Lord and Savior.

I invite you into my heart, and I run into your heart that overflows with love and forgiveness.

I love you, Jesus!

Date I said this prayer:

If you said this prayer for the first time, you have just invited Jesus into your heart and chosen Him as the Lord of your life. You are on your way to the destiny that He has for you!

```
Do you not feel it?
Do you not perceive?
The power of destiny sweeping through your heart?
```

Destiny Awaits:

What *Destiny Awaits* chapter impacted you the most and why?

What three take-aways can you immediately apply to your life after going through the *Destiny Awaits* journey?

1.)

2.)

3.)

Your Destiny Awaits Prayer Response:

For although we live in the natural realm, we don't wage a
military campaign employing human weapons, using manipulation to
achieve our aims. Instead, our spiritual weapons are energized
with divine power to effectively dismantle the defenses behind
which people hide. We can demolish every deceptive fantasy that
opposes God and break through every arrogant attitude that is
raised up in defiance of the true knowledge of God. We capture,
like prisoners of war, every thought and insist that it bow in
obedience to the Anointed One. Since we are armed with such
dynamic weaponry, we stand ready to punish any trace of rebellion,
as soon as you choose complete obedience.
2 Corinthians 10:3, 5-6 (TPT)

Xixty Cowa Tyim ... Destined to Overcome!

Notes

THE CURSE

1   Nathan Wagner, dir. *"You"*, *YouTube*. *17* Jan. 2020.https://youtu.be/wOTMpLXBa8c.

FAITH

2   Psychology Today, Adrian R. Camilleri Ph.D.
     Life's Biggest Decisions, January 31, 2021

THE POWER OF ENCOURAGEMENT

3   Nathan Wagner, dir. "Eyes of Love", *YouTube*. 17 Jan. 2018.https://youtu.be/b5x6qQyzX2U.

LIGHT

4   Nathan Wagner, dir. "Light", *YouTube*. 8 Jan 202. https://youtu.be/U4x3cPzOy9c.

5   Nathan Wagner, dir. "Light", *YouTube*. 8 Jan 202. https://youtu.be/U4x3cPzOy9c.

Made in the USA
Monee, IL
03 March 2022

92176905R00089